Sustainable Profitability in a Disrupted Legal Market

Authors
Norman K Clark and Lisa M Walker Johnson

Managing director
Sian O'Neill

Sustainable Profitability in a Disrupted Legal Market
is published by

Globe Law and Business Ltd
3 Mylor Close
Horsell
Woking
Surrey GU21 4DD
United Kingdom
Tel: +44 20 3745 4770
www.globelawandbusiness.com

Printed and bound by CPI Group (UK) Ltd, Croydon CR0 4YY, United Kingdom

Sustaining Profitability in a Disrupted Legal Market

ISBN 9781787422667
EPUB ISBN 9781787422674
Adobe PDF ISBN 9781787422681
Mobi ISBN 9781787422698

Table of contents

Seismic shifts in the legal services industry

1. Introduction

The legal services industry is changing; and for most law firms the greatest challenge of all is to remain competitive and profitable in legal markets that are being disrupted by unprecedented levels of competition. Purchasers of legal services, sophisticated and otherwise, are demanding better and more responsive service, and legal expertise tailored to their specific situations and objectives. They demand more but increasingly are unwilling to pay more. Advanced law practice technology and the introduction of artificial intelligence into law firms are accelerating this process by creating higher expectations.

2. Will the law firm of the future be a computer?

This report is about law firm profitability, not artificial intelligence; but the impact of advanced technology and artificial intelligence cannot be ignored. Inexpensive global technology has become the most significant factor in the disruption of the legal services industry. It also is the most important factor in developing a strategy for sustainable profitability in any law firm, regardless of size, location or practice specialty. Artificial intelligence is not just a bigger, faster computer. Its distinguishing characteristic is its ability to learn, in other words to perform many – perhaps most – of the tasks currently performed by highly paid lawyers. Artificial intelligence will be as much a part of the law firm of the future as desks and paper.

Sustainable Profitability in a Disrupted Legal Market

So, will the law firm of the future be a computer? No, but technology will fundamentally change the way that legal service providers make money.

The World Economic Forum has published an important article on the impact of automation on jobs in the mid-2010s. It has important implications for law firms, especially small ones. In "One. That's how many careers automation has eliminated in the last 60 years",[1] Sarah Kessler points out that only one of the 270 occupations listed in the 1950 US Census has since been eliminated by automation: elevator operator. However, a McKinsey study suggests that automation could replace up to 35% of professional services jobs.[2]

Notwithstanding increased awareness in the legal profession of the threats and, more importantly, the opportunities that advanced technology and artificial intelligence present, the dominant responses amongst law firms worldwide continue to be denial, distinguishing and deferral.

Typical reactions to advanced technology and artificial intelligence
- **Denial:** The legal profession is fundamentally different from elevator operators and factory workers. This will not affect us very much.
- **Distinguishing:** This will affect the big firms, but not small ones like us. This is probably important in big markets like the US or the UK, but it will not have much impact in a small market like ours. This will affect law firms with commodity practices like intellectual property or collections; but it will not significantly change the way that high-end legal services like ours are delivered.
- **Deferral:** We will figure out what we need to do when the need arises, probably five or 10 years from now.

As Brian Sheppard of the Seton Hall University School of Law observed in 2015, this reaction is not surprising, especially because of the perceived threat to traditional levels of law firm profitability:

It should come as no surprise that many legal services providers are wary of these innovations. Not only must they cope with clients who are unwilling to pay pre-recession rates, they might eventually have to contend with competition from non-lawyers and machines. Some commentators suspect that lawyers, at least certain types of lawyers, could become extinct.[3]

Responses by managing partners and chairpersons of 398 US law firms, including 45% of the 500 largest, to a survey conducted in 2018 reveal that even in the face of unmistakably disruptive changes in the legal market, most law firms are reluctant to change. In 69% of law firms, partners resist most change efforts. The survey report comments:

> *Clearly, there was no extinction event that made law firms irrelevant after the recession ... Few firms have taken full advantage of the disruption as an opportunity to run with it to distinguish themselves from competitors. Being a thought leader and early adopter of new methodologies and technologies is a clear differentiator that few law firms have embraced.*[4]

All this leads to four important forecasts concerning the impact of legal practice technology and artificial intelligence on law firm operations and continued profitability, not far in the future but now:

- **Law firms should look at artificial intelligence as a tool to improve productivity, not just operating costs.** As with traditional approaches to work process re-engineering in law firms, the principal effects that artificial intelligence will have

"Inexpensive global technology has become the most significant factor in the disruption of the legal services industry. It also is the most important factor in developing a strategy for sustainable profitability."

on the profitability of law firms will come from greater fee-earner productivity, especially for partners and other senior lawyers, rather than from reduced costs. Significant cost reductions will happen, but it is exponentially increased productivity that will have the greater impact on profitability.

- **Most jobs in law firms will not be eliminated, but they will be transformed.** Law firms that assume that artificial intelligence will eliminate some clerical and administrative jobs are, at best, only half-correct. Many of the functions now performed by junior associates, trainees and paralegals, such as research, preliminary analysis of a matter and document preparation, will be substantially reduced almost to the point of elimination. Computers will not replace these junior fee earners, but they could reduce the number that a law firm will need to maintain profitable workflow leverage. They will also change the skills that all lawyers in a firm, but especially associates, will need to remain relevant to the delivery of legal services.
- **To get the most benefit from artificial intelligence, law firms must rethink their assumptions about how they manage the preparation and delivery of legal services to clients.** Automating an inefficient, marginally profitable work process

"The six drivers represent a portal to a deeper understanding of the unique situation, culture, and operational habits of each law firm, not only explaining the challenges but also charting a course to sustainable improvements."

does not make it better, only faster. This is why it usually is better first to examine and understand fully the current levels of, and weaknesses in, the profitability of the firm's practice groups and client services. In other words, fix the problems in the existing processes before applying the technology. Don't expect the technology to solve the problems by itself.

- **The total return on investment, both tangible and intangible, in artificial intelligence might be highest for small and midsize firms.** This is because of its potential to help these firms remain competitive and profitable, especially in the retail sector of the legal services industry and in price-sensitive practice areas.

The most important thing is to start now to consider how artificial intelligence and other improvements in information technology and communications are beginning not only to disrupt business as usual in legal markets, but also to transform the traditional law firms that are trying to compete in them. If you wait for the 'law firm of the future' to arrive, it will be too late ever to catch up.

3. A diagnostic approach

Although the shape and direction of the legal services industry over the next five to 10 years are not certain, this report suggests a flexible, diagnostic strategy not only to protect the profitability of any law firm, practice group or solo practice, but also to assure that it can be sustained despite the disruptive changes that are likely to continue to shake the foundations of the industry.

A two-part strategy for sustainable profitability
- **Back to basics – but in a new way.** It is easy for panic to supplant reason when a traditional law firm faces new challenges that might be beyond the lawyers' professional experience. "I was trained to be a lawyer, not a robot operator," one partner commented recently. The authors advocate a diagnostic approach based on the six classic drivers of law firm profitability, which allow lawyers to identify promptly, define and diagnose accurately and respond effectively to specific profitability issues before they degrade into a financial crisis (see the following chapter).
- **Change readiness.** Even when a law firm is aware of the need to change, can the leaders of the firm actually do it? The authors urge a new approach to managing the adjustments that a law firm will need to respond effectively to disruptive changes in the legal markets in which it competes.

The traditional forces that have shaped law firm profitability for the past 200 years are still present and will remain relevant in the future; but they need to be understood and directed in new ways that are better suited to the seismic shifts that are beginning to shake the legal services industry today and will continue to do so for the foreseeable future. The six drivers represent a portal to a deeper understanding of the unique situation, culture, and operational habits of each law firm, not only explaining the challenges but also charting a course to sustainable improvements.

Although they are a set of valuable diagnostic tools, the insights derived from the six classic drivers of profitability do not constitute a cure. Understanding the causes and planning clever responses and improvements are good starts towards better profitability; but sustainable results – ones that will withstand future disruptions in the legal market – also require an alert, always inquiring management of the profound changes in the way a law firm, or even a solo practice, operates. These changes, the ones that must occur inside each firm if it is to remain a viable enterprise, might be the greatest disruptions of all.

The six classic drivers

1. Introduction

The six factors that have traditionally exercised the greatest overall influence on the profitability and long-term financial performance of law firms worldwide are discussed below. The relative impact of each of these 'six classic drivers' varies from firm to firm; however, the solution to profitability problems in a law practice – whether short-term or chronic – is almost always found in one or more of them.

The six classic drivers
- pricing;
- productivity;
- realisation;
- cost management;
- staff compensation; and
- leverage.

2. Old questions turned upside down

Traditionally, each of the six classic drivers has posed an implicit question that leads to some form of assumed best practice in the management of law firm profitability. That said, the disruption of legal markets now underway is disrupting the basic assumptions on which the six drivers themselves are based. It might seem paradoxical, but one of the principal effects of recent disruption of the legal services industry is that, although the basic questions and assumptions underpinning much of the traditional thinking about law firm profitability are being challenged, the usefulness of the six classic drivers as practical insight-producing analytical processes is perhaps greater than ever before.

We must reframe the questions that we used to ask about profitability from a different – and, for some lawyers, uncomfortable – perspective. It is much like looking through the telescope from the other end.

2.1 Pricing: are you charging a high enough fee?

Historically, this has been the key issue in pricing legal services, and since the late 1990s – especially since 2010 – law firms worldwide have encountered strong price resistance from clients across the spectrum of commercial legal services.[5] This trend has been stimulated further by predatory pricing[6] by non-traditional competitors, such as foreign law firms, entering a traditional legal market. Even new clients now expect discounts that were formerly reserved for the firm's best clients.

Today, the question of pricing is no longer asked from the law firm's perspective, but that of the client: *Is the firm charging a fee that is low enough?*

2.2 Productivity: are our fee earners fully utilised with billable work?

Imbalances in fee-earner utilisation has long been a substantial problem in many, perhaps most, law firms. Of all the various ways to measure the overall contribution and worth of a law firm associate, billing has been assumed in most firms to be the most important. Billable hours have traditionally driven almost all decisions made about associates: promotion, compensation, work assignments, and even whether an associate should remain employed in the firm.

Things began to change in the late 1990s. As clients started to demand fixed fees rather than hourly rates for more complex legal work, the associate who recorded 2,200 billable hours was no longer necessarily a hero. Law firms also became aware of the 'overproductive partner' paradox, the partner who billed so many hours that other activities that usually have much greater long-term value for the firm, such as business development and the professional development of associates, received secondary priority or were not done at all. Law firms began to realise that the best use of a partner's time, perhaps the most valuable asset in any law firm, was not to sit at the desk grinding out billable hours.

As advanced technology enables lawyers to produce high-quality, accurate legal work faster, the exponentially greater work capacity of most law firm associates will outstrip the demand for their services. An associate will soon be able to produce three or four times the amount of work in a day that has been possible in the past. Because the demand for legal services is unlikely to keep pace with improvements in law practice technology, many law firms will find that they have too many associates. Instead of the average utilisation rate being in the vicinity of five to seven billable hours per day, the increased output potential of associates might reduce average utilisation to two or three hours per day, even when technology allows associates to produce much higher volumes of legal work in a shorter time.

Today, the productivity question is beginning to shift: *Do we have too many people and not enough technology to sustain our revenue goals?*

2.3 Realisation: what percentage of the billable work is actually collected?

Realisation rates have long been one of the basic diagnostic items in the conventional profitability management toolbox, but also one of the most unskilfully used. The authors believe that most law firms traditionally have been afraid to attempt the changes that an unsatisfactory realisation rate suggests.

"Law firms began to realise that the best use of a partner's time, perhaps the most valuable asset in any law firm, was not to sit at the desk grinding out billable hours."

As a result, many law firm partners shrug and accept a '90-90-90' set of realisation rates as business as usual. This means that they grudgingly accept collecting less than 73% of the fees that they have earned (90% recording realisation; 90% billing realisation; 90% collection realisation).[7]

Sophisticated purchasers of legal services are already increasingly intolerant of errors and rework that could have been avoided. In some firms, preventable rework, especially in document drafting and production, can account for as much as 70% of the write-offs or write-downs of billed work. As some firms introduce advanced technology and AI systems to control quality and reduce errors, they are developing strong competitive advantages in terms of being able to avoid write-offs. The money that is billed and collected through better realisation rates is almost pure profit.

More demanding client expectations and more intense competition continue to disrupt the legal services markets, and the resulting squeeze on profitability is driving law firms to investigate realisation not simply as a lost cost of doing business, but as perhaps one of the most important financial metrics to help sustain profitability in the future. The authors' recent experience advising law firms about

"Firms that are reluctant to make the frequently substantial financial investments in better technology, communications and client service now risk disqualifying themselves from achieving the long-term, sustainable increases in profitability that these efforts can produce."

profitability issues suggest that, especially with the application of more powerful law practice technology, it is possible for almost any law firm to increase realisation to almost 100%, falling short of that goal only because of single-incident human error.

So, the question now is: *What do we need to do to achieve and sustain virtual 100% realisation?*

2.4 Cost management: how well do you manage operating costs?

Lawyers, by training and professional prudence, tend to be wary of risks, especially those for which some of the major factors appear uncertain or are even unknown. Too often, however, this results in reluctance to make the investments that are needed to support continued financial performance and long-term growth.

For as long as the prevailing cost-management paradigm was to control and, when possible, reduce operating costs, this investment reluctance usually did not do much harm. Once in a while, risk-averse partners might have passed up what could have been a good business opportunity; but the firm remained on solid financial ground.

Firms that are reluctant to make the frequently substantial financial investments in better technology, communications and client service now risk disqualifying themselves from achieving the long-term, sustainable increases in profitability that these efforts can produce. In other words, by saving money now, overly investment-averse law firms will almost certainly suffer greater opportunity costs later.

The greater risk – and sometimes a potentially lethal one – is not making the necessary investments. So, the cost-management question has become: *How good is your return on investment in operating costs?*

2.5 Staff compensation: are your fee earners paid more than they produce?

With advanced technology, the answer is likely to become "No". To function at a minimum acceptable level of profitability, associates and paralegals will need to master new knowledge and skills in the management and operation of legal technology in an environment of accelerating technological advances and the increased importance of legal technology in their work. Law firm leaders and managers should start now to rethink, at a very fundamental level, how many and what kinds of traditionally functioning associates they will need in their firms. The basic relationship between junior fee earners and their firms is going to change dramatically, as technology will enable a law firm to outsource substantially all the traditional functions currently performed in-house by associates.

In this technology-driven practice environment, the level of compensation paid to each paralegal or associate is becoming increasingly irrelevant. Law firms will pay what they need to pay to recruit and retain people who have the right blend of legal knowledge and technology-related skills. As productivity increases for associates, and non-lawyers begin to take over many of the functions previously performed only by associates or, in some cases, only by partners, well-managed firms will experience a levelling in their staffing requirements and, in many firms, a reduction in the number of non-partner fee earners they will need to handle the demand for legal services. Law firms can also expect to see a substantial increase in the outsourcing of legal service functions previously performed in-house.

So, even as the average compensation paid to an associate, for example, might increase to compensate for higher skills, this rise will be offset by a much greater reduction in the overall personnel costs. The new question in terms of staff compensation becomes: *How can we reduce our total spending – in-house and outsourced – for functions currently performed by our associates?*

2.6 Leverage: is your ratio of associates to partners too high to be profitable?

Many lawyers can remember the times in the 20th century when one partner frequently was supported by two or three secretaries. Today that ratio has flipped, with one secretary typically supporting two or three partners. Traditional concepts of staffing leverage, with their assumptions about the most profitable ratio of associates to partners, are being turned upside down and becoming increasingly irrelevant. As technology enables associates to perform many of their traditional functions 10 or 20 times faster, and with exponentially greater accuracy and analytical quality, a staffing ratio of four associates to one partner, instead of being reasonably profitable, could become quite unprofitable.

It has been challenging enough in the past for partners to manage and supervise four or five associates, ensuring that their work is performed profitably and at consistently high levels of professional quality. Imagine the challenge today, when a partner must manage work output equivalent to that of 40 or 50 associates.

The role of leverage in law firm profitability is changing. The traditional method of measurement – the associate-to-partner staffing ratio – is quickly becoming obsolete, because it no longer accurately approximates to how the legal work in a practice group or team flows amongst partners and associates.[8]

The other, more accurate, method of measurement – workflow leverage – is replacing staffing ratios in some law firms as the principal

"As technology enables associates to perform many of their traditional functions 10 or 20 times faster, and with exponentially greater accuracy and analytical quality, a staffing ratio of four associates to one partner, instead of being reasonably profitable, could become quite unprofitable."

leverage measurement. Workflow ratios are based on the relative amount of work performed by partners and associates, usually measured in billable hours (including in matters that are not billed on an hourly rate). However, workflow ratios are already becoming somewhat less accurate as the traditional concept of the billable hour becomes a less accurate way to measure the volume of work produced. For now, and into the foreseeable future, it appears likely that the billable hour, perhaps with some adjustments based on the extent to which the task was performed primarily by artificially intelligent systems, will remain the prevailing work unit, even if it never shows up on a bill to a client.

This possibility could turn the use of leverage as a profitability management tool upside down. Under the old paradigms, and within certain upper limits that depended on the nature of the tasks performed, the higher the workflow leverage the better. In the future, law firms can expect to see leverage becoming an alarm setting rather than a threshold for improved profitability. Very high workflow leverage ratios could become a threat to profitability if the transition to advanced technology and AI is not accompanied by equally sophisticated quality-assurance systems and processes. Partners will be challenged to keep up with the tidal wave of work produced by associates and their new electronic "colleagues".

The new basic question for leverage will be: *Is your ratio of associates to partners too high to assure consistently high quality?*

3. Diagnostic tools in a change-ready professional culture

This report not only revisits the basic concepts of the six classic drivers of law firm profitability, illustrating how they remain useful in a disrupted legal services industry, but also demonstrates their use as diagnostic tools that can produce insights into the most frustrating problems in law firm profitability. In recent years, the legal profession has finally been awakened by the seismic rumblings in the rest of the business world.

"The law firm of the future" has become a popular topic in blogs, articles, and conferences. This report seeks to supply an essential element that appears to be largely absent from most of these discussions: diagnostics. It is not an attempt to explain what is happening to law firm profitability, but rather how to diagnose and respond to the profitability issues arising from a disrupted legal market and a legal services industry that is beginning to undergo fundamental change.

In this regard, there really is not much utility in attempting to retreat to the basics by which law firms have operated for the past 200 years or more. However, the basic tools of profitability, applied in ways that are adapted to the new business environment of the legal services industry, can stimulate insights, support well-informed decisions, and serve as catalysts for results that can withstand the disruptions that are likely to continue. Wielded with skill in a professional culture that embraces change rather than resists it, these tools will produce the sustainable profitability and business confidence that traditional law firms will need as they try to navigate the challenging and still largely unexplored terrain ahead – and over the horizon.

Pricing –
classic driver #1

1. A thought experiment: £10 per hour

The general counsel of one of your firm's largest and oldest clients tells you that she has been directed by her board to reduce legal spending. She hands you a schedule of the new fixed fees that her company is willing to pay.

"The good news," she says, "is that you will get substantially more work from us – all of our acquisitions and competition law work. In addition, we will start sending you more of our tax work."

"Do we have any negotiating room for some of these fees?" you ask. "They look much lower than we have been charging your company in the past."

"No, sorry," she replies. "There's no room for negotiation, I'm afraid, unless you want to propose a lower price. And I can tell you, in confidence, that several other law firms – ones that we haven't used in the past – have already approached us to offer fees that are significantly lower than these."

Back at the office, you retrieve the billing records for your client's account for the past five years. You do some quick calculations based on the recorded hours for the various types of matter. You realise that, if you agree to the client's new fee schedule, you will be doing the work for an average of less than £10 per hour.

You and your partners believe that the client is too important, both to your firm and in the business community, for your firm to give up the relationship. From your long association with the general counsel, you are convinced that she is being truthful when she says that there is no possibility of negotiating higher fees.

Is there a way that your firm can deliver these legal services for an average of less than £10 per hour?

2. Are your fees low enough to be competitive and high enough to be profitable?

This question describes the profitability squeeze that most law firms, especially small and midsize ones, find themselves in today. Even worse, there are no signs in most of the legal markets in the world that the pressure is going to lessen.

Traditionally, pricing was one of the most powerful forces in law firm profitability. In many law firms, the prevailing assumption was, *If we charge a high enough fee, we are assured of making a nice profit.*

Around 30 or 40 years ago, law firms could count on client ignorance as a profit centre. Fee proposals were seldom challenged, and in some jurisdictions a lawyer who habitually offered below-market rates could be sanctioned for unethical conduct. Large, sophisticated in-house legal departments tended to be small and highly dependent on outside counsel for representation and advice in complex matters. A second prevailing assumption for many law firms was, *The client usually will pay whatever we charge.*

These two assumptions have been swept away in the 21st century. Pricing characteristics of disrupted markets are becoming part of the normal dynamic in the legal services industry. Previously unusual, isolated phenomena have become familiar to most law firms:

- New clients, with no prior relationship with the firm, expect a significant discount for a single matter, while vaguely alluding to the faintest prospects of future work.
- Clients demand volume discounts without ever delivering any volume work.
- Predatory pricing by non-traditional legal service providers have sparked all-out price wars in some markets among otherwise conservative law firms, and a financial race to the bottom that hurts all the participants.
- Price sensitivity in some traditionally high-volume or commodity

practice areas, such as trademarks, collections, and asset recovery, has a carry-over effect, stimulating greater price consciousness for legal services that previously had been relatively price-insensitive.

Although increasingly price-sensitive, clients are not suckers for any low price. They are not fooled, at least not for long, by a discount from an artificially high "standard" rate that nobody charges. In this climate, there is a strong temptation simply to compete, at least temporarily, on price. Slash your fees to the lowest possible level. Distinguish yourself as the cheapest provider in your market.

3. Low pricing: an unsustainable strategy

In fact, low pricing is not a strategy at all; but that is not to say that it is irrelevant or can be ignored, as any law firm that has recently competed in a "beauty contest" knows very well.

The illusion of having a competitive advantage because you charge the lowest price soon evaporates even in the most price-competitive markets. All that it takes is for a competitor to offer fees that are slightly less than yours – sometimes only £10 less – and whatever competitive advantage you had from being the cheapest provider

"A low-price advantage can easily be trumped by other, more important, service considerations like responsiveness or understanding of the client's business."

in the market is lost (unless, of course, you are so foolish as to reduce your rates even further).

Moreover, a low-price advantage can easily be trumped by other, more important, service considerations like responsiveness or understanding of the client's business.

Since 2002, the authors' consulting firm has conducted confidential surveys of decision makers and influencers in the client organisations of law firms worldwide.[9] Survey respondents are asked to evaluate the relative importance of 20 indicators of quality in legal services. On price, for example, respondents are asked to respond to the statement, *The firm charges the lowest fees among law firms that I consider to be credible competitors for my legal work*, by selecting from five possible choices as to relative importance:

- **Decisive:** I will not hire a law firm that cannot meet my needs and expectations in this area; and I will not continue to use a law firm that fails in this area.
- **Important:** I consider this factor when selecting a law firm, but it is not decisive.
- **Secondary:** I usually do not consider this indicator when selecting a law firm. I can excuse occasional failure to meet my expectations in this area.
- **Unimportant:** I never consider this factor in selecting a law firm or in evaluating the quality of legal services that I receive.
- **No opinion/not applicable.**

Overall, low price ranks 16th out of the 20 factors in terms of perceived importance, with a consensus that it is, at best, a secondary factor. In the sixteen years during which the authors have been conducting this survey, low price has never ranked within the top 10, even among the clients of firms that offer low-cost services in commodity practice areas.

The authors conclude that, at best, the price quoted for legal services is important only to the extent that, to be competitive, a firm must offer a price that is within a reasonable range of offerings by credible service providers. Once a firm's quoted fee is within the competitive range, factors other than low price govern the client's selection.

What, then, are these new indicators of value in legal services? The authors' research, described above, has found that, among the 20 factors that are presented in their survey of decision makers and influences in client organisations, low price was one of the least important.

In the past 20 years, as one practice area after another has become more price-sensitive, most law firms have had to choose between what appeared to be equally bad options. Some firms simply withdrew from the competition or spun off low-profitability, high-volume practices such as trademarks administration and collections into separate, highly leveraged and reasonably profitable business units. Firms that stayed in low-price service areas had to overhaul their internal work processes, service delivery systems and administrative structure in order to lower their operating costs to within a price range that was competitive and at least marginally profitable. In some instances, even these efforts to manage at bare bones cost levels were inadequate, because the volume that the firm needed to produce a consistent level of revenue necessary to allow operations on such thin profit margins never materialised.

Loss leader strategies have also been largely disappointing. Under a loss leader strategy, a firm delivers some legal services at a loss in order to retain clients that offer the high-value corporate work the firm really wants. However, most law firms that have attempted loss leader strategies, especially since 2010, have been disappointed by the results. The lower prices have not led new clients to the firm; or, where they have, few clients have "upgraded" to the higher-value cases and transactions that the firm hoped to capture. In retrospect, partners often had overly optimistic expectations about an existing client's predisposition to remain with the firm simply because of a low-price service the firm offered in addition to the higher-value commercial legal work. In other words, the firm would probably have kept the high-value work without delivering lower-value services at a loss.

4. Are your fees high enough?
Rather than joining the local price war, might you not actually need to raise some of your fees?

In emerging markets in Africa, Latin America and Asia, as well as in more mature markets in Europe and North America, it is not uncommon to discover that a law firm has not adjusted its fees in the past three to four years. Previously, there was great concern among law firm managers and management consultants, like the authors, when fees that once were market average dropped below the median, while the market's tolerance for (although not necessarily its pleasure about) higher legal fees moved upward. But in most practice areas and legal markets more recently, and especially since 2010, the concern about outdated fee schedules is that, rather than being lower than what the legal market will accept, they have remained too high still to be competitive.

Sometimes law firms are unaware of changing fee tolerances in a disrupted legal market until it is almost too late, perhaps due to a

"Fully loaded operating cost, especially when computed as an hourly average, is a simple measurement, easily within the capability of any law firm; but it remains largely unknown or ignored."

reluctance on the part of some lawyers to discuss fees with their clients. One thing is clear, however. The old assumption – *With a fee this high we must be making a profi*t – is no longer a reliable basis for the pricing of legal services.

Of course, every law firm should review its fees every year to confirm that its standard rates are consistent with the rates actually charged to clients. In this regard, it is not unusual to find that nobody in a law firm actually charges standard rates at all. An annual review of fee discussions with clients and prospective clients, supported by the experiences of the partners and external market intelligence, is also important to ensure that the fees are competitive.

It is vital, therefore, to maintain pricing policies and practices that are flexible enough to remain within the competitive range in a fast-changing legal market; but it also has become more important to confirm each year that the firm's basic assumptions about pricing, and especially about discounting as a client relations or business development tactic, continue to produce a reliable, sustainable profit margin for each matter and, when possible, for each hour of fee-earner work. Without this type of disciplined review, a law firm risks being surprised when it wins an attractive matter but then loses a lot of money on it.

Pricing and cost management, the fourth of the six classic drivers, are more interlinked in law firm profitability than ever before. As discussed in 'Cost management – classic driver #4', one of the most important profitability measurements is fully loaded operating cost or FLOC.

How much does it cost your firm or your practice group to produce one hour of legal services? Surprisingly, many firms don't know the answer to this basic question. Fully loaded operating cost, especially when computed as an hourly average, is a simple measurement, easily within the capability of any law firm; but it remains largely unknown or ignored. In a few cases in the authors' experience, management have even declined to report it for fear that it would be internally divisive among partners in different practice groups. Nonetheless, even if the numbers are not as complete or precise as one would like, every law firm needs to know its profit point. Only then will partners be ready to discuss fees intelligently with their clients. Without this information, fee quotations – even hourly rates – are little more than hopeful guesswork.

5. Value, not price

Pricing operates somewhat differently in purchasing decisions by current or recent clients than it does for prospective clients. With very few exceptions, price will not be a decisive factor for prospective clients. Rather, price represents a range of competitive and credible fee proposals by law firms.

For most current or recent clients, the price charged becomes a factor only to the extent that it helps to define the overall value that a law firm delivers. The authors' research and observations have established what most law firm partners know almost instinctively – that clients who have had satisfactory experiences with a law firm have a strong predisposition to return. Normally, when current or recent clients complain about fees they are really complaining about perceived value: they are not saying, *This is an outrageous fee!* but *I received outrageously poor value for what I paid.*

As noted previously, low price is at best a secondary factor in the decision to select a law firm or to continue to instruct that firm. Few law firms lose a good client solely due to high fees. Client surveys conducted by the authors' consulting firm demonstrate that an existing professional relationship – not price – is the top consideration in selecting a law firm for all but the most routine legal services.[10] Purchasers of legal services, including high-volume services, report that a price increase may be the stated excuse to fire a law firm; but that the real reasons almost always arise from dissatisfaction with other indicators of service quality. Price is simply the final straw.

"It has always been a good result when the value conversation leads a client to conclude: This firm is expensive but worth it. *In disrupted legal markets today, expensive* may *be hoping for too much; but* worth it *should still be the goal."*

What, then, are these other indicators, which combine to form a client's perception of value? Five critical indicators of quality – and therefore value in that context – in legal services have emerged from the authors' research, which are listed in order of relative importance, determined by an average weighted score from a survey of 6,623 respondents:

The five main indicators of quality in legal services
1. **Responsiveness:** The lawyers respond to telephone calls and emails as promptly as I require.

2. **Availability:** A partner is available to advise me when I need one.

3. **Committedness:** The lawyers in the firm demonstrate that they are committed to my success.

4. **Business understanding:** The firm's lawyers have a basic working knowledge of the factors that produce success in my business and they understand the business objectives in each case or transaction.

5. **Practical advice:** The firm provides advice that is not only legally correct but practical to implement in my business.[11]

6. An agenda for a value conversation

The most effective starting point for a conversation about value is to recognise that clients face the same or analogous profitability pressures in their own businesses and personal lives. They understand that most legal services are not like consumer electronics; they do not expect prices to drop forever. A client may bargain hard, but he or she still expects the lawyer to earn a reasonable profit. It has always been a good result when the value conversation leads a client to conclude: *This firm is expensive but worth it.* In disrupted legal markets today, *expensive* may be hoping for too much; but *worth it* should still be the goal.

The big pricing challenge for law firms in disrupted legal markets is to lead clients to think about value instead of price, that is, the return on their investment in legal services, and not the price of that investment. Consider questions like these:

6.1 What will be the total cost to the client?

Law firms that can still charge hourly rates are sometimes tempted to compensate for low hourly rates by recording more hours. Clients quickly see that they are being misled, paying a higher total cost than a firm with a higher hourly rate but that bills fewer hours, or a firm that charges a fixed fee. If the total legal cost for a matter is important to a client – and it usually is – a law firm should try to demonstrate, not just assert, how they can deliver all the components of a matter at a reasonable total cost to the client, with no contingencies, add-ons or other billing surprises.

Law firm partners must be prepared to talk in detail about the bottom line. For example, one small law firm won almost all of a major energy company's litigation simply by having the courage to review the two competitors' invoices. Even though the firm's partners charged hourly rates that were 10% to 15% higher than those charged by the competitors, the firm was able to demonstrate how well-managed delegation of work to associates and more efficient use of partner time would have produced total legal costs in the matters that they reviewed that were almost 25% lower than the two "low-cost" firms.

How could this firm do this? They had confidence in their ability to perform the client's work efficiently, at a low FLOC per fee-earner hour, and with quality assurance procedures that reduced lawyer time that was wasted by unbillable rework to correct mistakes. Regardless of the specific strategies and tactics that a law firm uses to build sustainable profitability, the more confident it is about the profitability of the agreed fee, the easier it becomes to set a fee – whether fixed or hourly – that lower-priced competitors might assume to be impossible to offer.

"Unprofitable clients are gluttonous consumers of law firm resources, especially partner time."

In other words, if it is so minded, a law firm can engage in near-predatory pricing and be profitable at the same time.

6.2 What is the true return on the client's investment?

Many low-price competitors never discuss concepts of value with their clients, only price. High-volume legal services tend to be relatively simple transactions, delivered in a routine way. Each one might be insignificant to the overall business success or long-term growth of the client. In a legal market in which everyone is charging approximately the same price for similar services, how can a law firm stand out from the competition, offering added value rather than low price?

Achieving this objective requires that law firms invest significant time and effort in gaining an in-depth understanding of a client's business goals, not just in a single matter but overall. *Understands my business* is consistently one of the top five quality indicators for law firm clients. Law firms that score the highest marks for understanding a client's business universally display three characteristics:

Characteristics of firms that understand the client's business

- They invest substantial partner time and attention in developing a thorough understanding of the strategic aspirations, business objectives, and internal operations of each client, even if it might not immediately appear to be relevant to the matter at hand.
- The firm's marketing team spends a significant amount of time compiling market intelligence about a client's industry sector, and not just trying to sell the firm.
- Knowledge about the client's business is shared, as appropriate, with associates and other staff members who have contact with the client.

6.3 Is it time to gently say goodbye?

If a client – even a longstanding and faithful one – refuses to be educated by a value conversation and insists that low price ranks above all other factors, continuation of the client relationship at bargain basement rates will probably hurt the law firm's long-term business interests. Unprofitable clients are gluttonous consumers of law firm resources, especially partner time. Each hour spent working for a marginal client is an hour that is forever lost for more profitable work or for business development.

This does not mean that a firm should automatically dump all marginally profitable clients. There may be solid business reasons for keeping marginal clients who offer:

- the long-term prospect of more profitable work (a speculative proposition in most cases); or
- the potential to refer other, more profitable, clients.

Some law firms treat the losses incurred by continuing to serve an unprofitable client as a marketing investment; but as with all marginal investments, the partners serving that client must remain alert to the dangers of sunk-cost bias: *We have invested so much time, effort and resources in this client relationship, we cannot walk away now.* Sunk-cost bias usually only renders an already unprofitable financial relationship more so.

7. Escaping the squeeze

Law firms often feel pressure from two directions, with the firm trapped in the middle:

- **Whatever you charge today will be too much tomorrow.** With exceptions that are too few and too specialised to offer real hope, the downward pressure on legal fees is going to continue and intensify as even previously price-insensitive sectors of the legal market become more price conscious.
- **Whatever you deliver today will be too little tomorrow.** Simply stated, clients want more – more responsiveness, more service quality, and value-added advice beyond what most law firms considered to be the scope of legal services 20 years ago.

Law firms of all sizes – and especially small and midsize firms that appear to have less tolerance for these pressures than big firms – can escape this squeeze. First, they must continue to set fees based on each firm's profit goals, which might need to be lowered to meet market expectations, and internal operating costs, which if not managed creatively are likely to continue to grow. The unpleasant reality has emerged, especially since 2010, that in most legal markets fees are not likely to increase significantly in the future, other than in response to unusual levels of inflation. As a constant, the fees that clients are willing to pay has probably peaked. Therefore, law firms must end their traditional reliance on high fees to assure profitability and look for ways to improve productivity and reduce costs, without compromising client services.

Productivity –
classic driver #2

1. A thought experiment: the 80-hour day

What if, thanks to a combination of advanced technology and artificial intelligence, your personal productivity could increase tenfold? In other words, what if you could take just one hour to do work that previously took 10 hours? Or looking at it another way, what if you could reduce your work day from 10 or 12 hours and produce in an eight-hour day billable work that previously required 80 hours?

How would you reorganise your "80-hour" work day? Would you continue your previous work habits, grinding out as much billable work as you could in your time in the office in order to collect more fees? Or would your new levels of productivity allow you to spend more time in activities that, while not billable, produce greater long-term value for your firm?

2. Are you working too hard?

Productivity presents a paradox. Some partners in law firms are so productive as fee generators that they are actually unproductive in terms of long-range business results. They spend so much time doing billable legal work that there is no time left for other things, many of which have not only greater long-term importance but also short-range financial value.

Although easy to tally in the traditional language of the billable hour, productivity might be the most difficult of the six classic drivers to manage well. So many complex internal relationships within the firm, such as the habitual delegation of work from partners to associates, affect productivity. It also calls to account the cultural assumptions of the partnership, such as the traditional view that the hardest-working lawyers are also the most valuable and, especially since the early 2000s, the question of where the firm should set the balance between financial reward and quality of personal life.

3. Is the billable hour obsolete?

Although not perfect, the billable hour has traditionally been the most practical way to measure productivity in law firms. Most lawyers are comfortable with it. However, given the pressures on profitability imposed by disrupted legal markets, the way in which the billable hour has been managed in many firms has been deeply flawed.

Some firms continue to equate billable hours with productivity, assuming that there is a direct correlation between number of billable hours recorded and profitability. In these firms, the first reaction to downward pressure on fees is to exhort the fee earners to "work harder" – defined as recording more billable hours for more clients.

"The real value of the billable hour has moved in-house. What previously was a basic unit in the pricing of legal work is now a critically important measurement of internal productivity."

This back-to-basics reaction is not universal, however. Some firms go to the other extreme, viewing the billable hour as irrelevant to their fee structures. The migration in many legal markets from hourly rates to non-hourly fee structures such as fixed fees, per-unit fees, and scale fees (ie, a percentage of the value of the case or transaction) has produced an assumption in some firms that the billable hour has become an irrelevant nuisance and, therefore, redundant as a measurement of productivity. These firms fall back on fee collections or modelled profitability,[12] which indirectly measure the volume of work a lawyer produces; but these alternatives lack the diagnostic capabilities achieved by recording every hour of work regardless of whether it results, directly or indirectly, in a fee collected from a client. For example, almost all of the measurements that the authors recommend in subsequent sections of this report to monitor factors such as realisation, cost management, and leverage require accurate measurement of how fee earners spend their time. Without timekeeping, these measurements either become little more than guesswork, without any realistic grounding in the work that people actually do, or so hypothetical and complex that they are not of practical use.

The real value of the billable hour has moved in-house. What previously was a basic unit in the pricing of legal work is now a critically important measurement of internal productivity; and it remains an essential factor in the diagnostic measurements that law firms need to detect problems in productivity, understand them, and respond before the early indicators of a problem have degraded into a financial crisis. Nonetheless, many law firms that continue to record fee-producing work resist using the same method to record the unbilled work that the firm performs for clients, as well as other activities such as business development, professional development and general management. Why record time that is never going to be billed?

This thinking, which persists especially in small law firms and among solo practitioners, denies fee earners and managers a useful productivity tool that they could have at no significant additional cost. The additional time and effort needed to record the unbilled work is negligible. Moreover, easy-to-use internet-based time and billing systems that are designed for small practices are available through very low-cost subscriptions; and most of them are powerful enough to generate all the basic management reports that a small law practice needs.

Without reasonably accurate and complete records of all its activities, it is very difficult, and in some instances impossible, for a law firm to make informed decisions about issues such as the most cost-effective staffing ratios, delegation, and work pricing when clients want a mode of billing other than hourly rates. For those firms, setting a profitable non-hourly fee becomes little more than guesswork when based on productivity assumptions – *How much work it will take to earn the fee* – unsupported by accurate time records for similar tasks in similar matters. This is one reason why many law firms quite correctly perceive great risk when they are required to propose a fixed fee.

4. What is the magic number?

The introduction of advanced technology and the impending entry of artificial intelligence greatly complicate the traditional question, *How many billable hours should we require of our fee earners?* It is becoming increasingly difficult to set a sure universal standard for law firm productivity expressed in the traditional terms of the billable hour.

Productivity levels vary widely from one legal market to another. In some Latin American or Caribbean firms, for example, the authors have observed that the most productive lawyers in a firm, in terms of both revenue and profits, might record fewer than 1,500 billable hours per year. By contrast, ranges of 1,800 to 2,000 hours are not only common in similar firms in the United States and United Kingdom, but are frequently *de facto* minimum requirements for associates. In those firms the productivity figures for top producers often exceed 2,500 hours per year.

There simply is no reliable universal standard for productivity; but one of the characteristics that the authors have observed in a majority of the firms that chronically fail to meet revenue targets has been average fee-earner productivity of less than 1,000 hours per year. At that level, it is very difficult for any law firm to absorb the increasing client demands for lower fees and discounts that are characteristic of a highly competitive legal market – even before the disruptive effects of market entry by low-price non-traditional service providers. The margin is usually too slender to sustain long-term profitability and growth, especially if the underproductive firm must also contend with increasing operating costs in critical areas such as facilities, technology and staff.

The effect of relatively low productivity on profitability
The following example illustrates the importance of productivity in the context of the traditional configuration of the production of legal work in a law firm.

- A and B are two commercial law firms in the same market, competing for the same types of clients and delivering the same services.
- Each firm has 10 associates.

- In firm A, the 10 associates produce an average of 1,500 hours of billable work per year, for a total of 15,000 hours.
- In firm B, the 10 associates produce an annual average of 1,200 hours, for a total of 12,000 hours.
- Each firm charges approximately the same fees for similar matters.

In terms of raw productivity, firm A is 25% more productive than firm B. Firm A requires only eight lawyers to produce the same number of billable hours produced by all 10 lawyers in firm B. This means that firm B is paying the salary and support costs of two extra, and arguably unneeded, underproductive associates. If the average salary for associates at firm B is, for example, £60,000 per year, the firm is spending a minimum of £120,000 in compensation costs that it could avoid through greater productivity. The cost is even greater when considering per-capita support costs such as secretarial staff and office services.

This suggests a clear profitability imperative for firm B: to increase its average associate productivity up to the level of that in firm A. By doing so, its associates will produce additional fees at virtually no additional operating cost – almost pure profit!

The example does not, however, explain why productivity is lower at B than at A. Low productivity is likely the result of systemic practice management weaknesses such as poor business development, inadequate delegation of work and chronic overstaffing, rather than any defect in performance or work ethic. Merely ordering the associates to produce more billable hours, the approach still taken by many law firms, will not solve the problem.

So, what is the magic number for the two law firms in this little case study? In the traditional context, firm B should boost average annual billable hours per associate to match or exceed those of firm A – 1,500 billable hours per year.[13] In the context of a disrupted legal services industry, the answer is not so simple. Consider these questions:

- What if law firm B uses artificially intelligent systems to review documents in its due diligence services in support of mergers and acquisitions, which allow two associates to complete in less than one day a document review that the two associates from firm A would require one week to complete?
- What if firm B uses artificially intelligent litigation management systems to evaluate, research, and draft opinions and briefs in less than two hours of associate time, compared to 20 hours of associate time for firm A?
- What if an associate in firm B, supported by artificial intelligence, can evaluate a client's tax position, prepare an

opinion with a comprehensive in-depth presentation of options and alternatives, and generate the necessary documentation to the taxation authority in less than one hour, compared to the 10 to 15 billable hours that it might take an associate in firm A to complete the same work?

The traditional concept of the billable hour does not really answer any of these questions, nor the many others that one might anticipate based on the facts in this hypothetical comparison.

5. Variation in productivity

What is the value of the billable hour as a measurement of productivity in a disrupted legal market and the law firms that must compete within it? Consistent with the concept that the management value of the billable hour has moved in-house, the billable hour has become even more important as a diagnostic tool. However – and this is a vitally important point that many law firm managers miss – it is not the absolute number of billable hours that are significant in evaluating productivity, but the variation in those numbers. In other words, the insight comes from watching how the numbers move.

Indicators of distribution of work
- Which, if any, of a law firm's fee earners record more than 140% or less than 60%[14] of the average billable hours for their constituency (ie, partners, associates, of counsel lawyers, paralegals)? This can be a useful indicator of inefficient distribution of work among fee earners, as well as unprofitable delegation of work from partners to associates and non-lawyer fee earners.
- When, during the course of a fiscal year, or even better over three fiscal years, has the average number of billable hours per month exceeded 140% or been less than 60% of the monthly average? This can provide insight into natural cycles of the demand for legal services in a practice area.
- What have been the variations in average billable hours per month and per year among practice groups and among fee-earner constituencies in the firm? This can often be an indicator of inefficient distribution of work.

The absolute number of billable hours that a law firm's fee earners record does not really matter in disrupted legal service markets. The market no longer cares how much time is required to produce a legal service, any more than a purchaser of an automobile cares how much time it took to build the car. Instead, the traditional concept of billable hours has become one of the most important diagnostic measurements to understand the relationship of productivity to profitability.

"The market no longer cares how much time is required to produce a legal service, any more than a purchaser of an automobile cares how much time it took to build the car."

6. The overproductive partner

This discussion of productivity has focused primarily on associates. Associate profitability has emerged as one of the most prominent profitability issues for law firms in recent years, as associates have demanded higher pay but not necessarily for more work. Perhaps a greater productivity-related risk to profitability can be found in the phenomenon that the authors describe as the 'overproductive partner' syndrome. Two episodes within the authors' experience illustrate the conceptual boundaries that define this risk.

- Over lunch with the two senior partners of a 20-lawyer commercial firm, the partners complained about the "productivity" of associates who recorded fewer than 2,500 billable hours per year. "We always bill more than 3,000 per year; why can't they?" the senior partners asked. In the same conversation, the two senior partners observed that their revenue performance had been flat for the past three years: "We're not getting new clients, not even new business from some of the clients who have historically been our top fee producers."
- A partner in a 300-lawyer international firm confessed, "Perhaps my partners should penalise me in my compensation if I bill more than 1,500 hours per year. They could well ask, 'What should I be doing that is not getting done?'"

Productivity can be a paradox for partners. The partner who is working the hardest on day-to-day client work might be contributing the least to the long-term success of the firm. This "overproductive" partner can be an even greater threat to long-term performance than the apparently underproductive associate. He or she is certainly a greater risk to long-term profitability than the partner whose performance has declined due to personal problems or transition to retirement. A partner can be overproductive and underproductive – perhaps even counterproductive – all at the same time. It all turns on the question that the partner asked in the second example above: *What should I be doing that is not getting done?*

Comparing average billable hours of partners and associates is a reliable diagnostic for overproductive partners. In most law firms worldwide, associates produce a higher average of billable hours than partners. This reflects the substantial responsibilities that partners have for non-billable functions, such as marketing, firm or practice group management, and mentoring junior lawyers. When the numbers are inverted, so that partners are producing more billable hours on average than their associates, the firm is usually suffering from the overproductive partner syndrome. This inversion is, in the authors' experience, the most important diagnostic sign of

"Productivity can be a paradox for partners. The partner who is working the hardest on day-to-day client work might be contributing the least to the long-term success of the firm."

inadequate management of partner time and delegation to non-partner fee earners.

Although they are undoubtedly working hard and bringing in fees, overproductive partners are not using their time for the best long-term benefit of the firm. The authors' research in law firms worldwide supports the proposition that for every hour a partner invests in developing new business from existing clients, the firm can expect to gain an average of between 10 and 16 hours of new work.

Gearing up a partner's billable hours
- A partner personally bills 1,500 hours per year.
- That partner delegates 10% of those hours to an associate who can perform the same functions with an equivalent level of efficiency and professional quality.[15]
- The partner devotes the 150 "saved" hours to business development from existing clients.
- Based on the authors' research, each partner hour spent developing new matters from current or recent clients can produce 10 hours of new work for the firm.
- Therefore, delegating 150 hours of work to associates can produce the opportunity to secure at least 1,500 hours of billable work from new matters.

Now, let's apply some numbers.

- Assume that the partner's average fee yield per billable hour is £400.
- Assume that an associate's average fee yield per billable hour is £150.
- If the partner "keeps" those 150 hours that might otherwise have been delegated to associates – and, very importantly, assuming that the client is willing to pay partner rates for the work – the total possible revenue generated by the partner from those 150 hours will be £60,000.
- If the partner uses the "found" 150 hours delegated to associates to develop new business from existing clients, the possible additional revenue to the firm will be 1,500 hours of work at the associate level, which at £150 per hour is £225,000, more than three times what a partner could have produced by grinding out billable work him- or herself.
- Even if one adds a relatively high supervisory overhead of 20%, representing the time the partner must spend to ensure that the associate performs the delegated work properly, the extra revenue will still be £120,000 – a more than 2-to-1 net return on investment.

Pursuing greater profitability by demanding more billable hours is an illusory effort and, in some firms, a fool's errand. This becomes even more apparent when factoring in a disrupted legal market. The better strategy is usually to have partners spend less time, not more, racking up billable hours and more time producing long-term value for the firm.

One way to facilitate this badly needed transition to a new way of thinking about the relationship between billable hours and fee-earner productivity is to consider the more realistic productivity measurement of "revenue-generation hours", which includes time spent on marketing and business development.

For example, a partner might be required to produce 1,800 revenue-generation hours each year, of which at least 1,500 must be traditional billable hours. At least 200 must be devoted to approved marketing and business development activities. These 200 hours, which the partner previously devoted to billable work, will be delegated to associates. The remaining 100 hours may be devoted to either type of revenue-generating activity, at the partner's discretion. These goals should be documented in an individual business plan for each partner.

Each category of revenue-generation hours – billable work and business development – can be assigned a financial value that is based on the average fee yield per hour.

The value of business development hours
- A partner recorded 1,800 billable hours last year, which produced £720,000 in fee revenue. The value of each billable hour, for purposes of planning allocation of a partner's time, is £400 (£720,000 divided by 1,800 hours).[16]
- This year, that partner's plan is to record 1,500 billable hours which, at a planning value of £400 per hour, would produce a total fee revenue of £600,000 (£400 multiplied by 1,500 hours).
- If a firm assumes an average return on investment of 4-to-1 for the time a partner spends on business development activities,[17] the "planning value" of each business development hour is £1,600 (£400 per hour times a projected return on investment of 4). Thus, the potential total value of 200 partner business development hours is £320,000.

The estimate of £320,000 in new business for the firm does not take into account three qualifying factors. First, as with any fee revenue produced by billable work, not all of the revenue from the new matters will be realised in the same fiscal year in which the partner made the investment of time in business development.

Second, the estimated new revenue does not take into account a possible multiplier effect from the addition of new clients, who should have a strong propensity to recommend the firm to others. Suppose, for example, that a partner spends five hours developing a new client for the firm, who produces a 4-to-1 return on the value of that investment. This calculation does not include the possibility that the new client might recommend the firm to another new client, who might bring additional work to the firm.

Finally, and perhaps most importantly, the achievement of this potential must be supported by serious business development planning, the prudent investment of marketing and business development funds to support each partner's efforts, and a professional development initiative to assure that each partner has the skills that he or she needs to be successful. These are things that all law firms should already be doing, even if they never use the productivity planning method outlined above.

The 100 discretionary hours
- Let's assume that the partner in this example elects to use the 100 discretionary hours to perform regular billable work rather than business development. The potential revenue produced by those hours, for planning purposes, would be £40,000.
- The total anticipated value of the revenue produced by the partner would therefore be as much as £960,000, not counting the value of secondary referrals by new clients:
- £600,000 generated by the partner's 1,500 "budget" of billable hours;
- £320,000 produced as a result of the partner's business development efforts; and
- £40,000 produced by the partner's 100 discretionary hours.

Thus, by reallocating only 200 hours – 11% of the total hours worked – from billable hours to business development, the partner in this example can increase fee production by at least one-third.

7. Moving beyond the billable hour
The foregoing analyses from a traditional law firm environment are compelling enough, but they do not take account of the additional impact of advanced legal practice technology and, increasingly, as we approach the 2020s, of artificial intelligence.

Returning to the example above – the law firms A and B:

- Suppose that, with advanced legal practice technology, an associate in firm B can produce in one hour the volume of legal work that it takes an associate in firm A at least four hours to produce.

- Assume the average fee yield per associate hour in each firm is £150. This would be one of the basic factors that each firm would use to calculate fixed fees or, to the extent that each firm still uses hourly billing, the hourly fees that the firm charges.
- Using the two firms' average billable hours per associate, firm B, which appears to be a comparatively low-productivity firm using only the traditional concept of billable hours, actually is the more productive in terms of fee revenue. Working only an average of 1,200 billable hours per year, an associate in firm B produces the equivalent of 4,800 hours of billable work in firm A. Even assuming that a tech-savvy associate in B earns 50% more salary than an associate in A, the associates in firm B are much more profitable:
- An associate in firm A produces 1,500 billable hours per year with a fee value of £225,000. After deducting a salary of £60,000, and not including the operating costs allocated to each associate, this produces a profit of £165,000.
- An associate in firm B produces the equivalent of 4,800 billable hours (1,200 billable hours multiplied by a technology factor of 4) per year, with a total value of £720,000. Even after deducting a salary that is 150% of that of an associate in A – £90,000 – and not including the operating costs allocated to each associate,[18] the profit to the firm is £630,000.
- Thus, the "underproductive" associate in firm B is more than 380% more profitable than the "fully utilised" associate in firm A.

8. Disruptive productivity

To continue to be profitable and competitive in a disrupted legal market, law firms should consider new "disruptive" concepts of productivity. The traditional view that profitability is ultimately a partner's responsibility remains valid; but partners need to disrupt their own assumptions and thinking about productivity. Simply working harder, grinding out more billable hours, will not be enough; in fact, it probably never was. Instead, partners should continually ask the question: *Is this the most productive use of my time?*

Partners also must understand how they are going to manage the exponential increases in productivity that advanced legal practice technology and artificial intelligence are already beginning to produce in the preparation, quality control, and delivery of legal services. The traditional concept of the billable hour will remain useful as a measurement of productivity; but it will need to be extended and adjusted to focus on the production of business results, such as increased revenue in less time, rather than the amount of work needed to produce those results.

Notwithstanding the examples in this section of the report,

"The traditional view that profitability is ultimately a partner's responsibility remains valid; but partners need to disrupt their own assumptions and thinking about productivity."

productivity in a disrupted legal market is not just a more sophisticated exercise in numbers. Clear measurable standards for individual and group productivity remain important, perhaps more so than ever in small law firms and solo practices. However, rather than chasing benchmarks and best practices promoted by external sources, productivity planning and evaluation must include a realistic view of each firm's market and client base.

Equally important, the partners must pay attention to the balance between business necessities and respect for the personal and family lives of everyone in the firm. The ability of technology exponentially to increase productivity by simplifying previously time-consuming and error-prone tasks can make the much-discussed goal of work–life balance more achievable.

Advanced technology and new concepts of productivity are facilitators, not solutions, for sustainable profitability in a disrupted legal market, just as they were in traditional competitive environments in the industry. The most important factors in individual and group productivity will remain the climate and culture in which people must work. These are what drive strategies for better productivity in a law firm and inspire each person in a firm to internalise the challenging new goals that law firms must achieve to remain competitive.

Realisation – classic driver #3

1. A thought experiment: collecting every penny

Your law firm has done an admirable job of recording and measuring every billable hour. You know precisely the value of the work performed by every fee earner in your firm. You have very clear and, on paper at least, profitable fee agreements with each client and for each matter.

You are shocked to learn that your firm is collecting only 75% of the fees that you have agreed with your clients. What must your firm do to raise this rate to 100%?

2. Leaving money in the street

Realisation describes how much of a firm's labour is realised in the form of cash. Does every hour of billable work ultimately result in an hour's worth of fees? Improving the realisation rate of a law firm continues to be one of the most reliable ways to improve profitability and sustain it, even in uncertain times and disrupted legal markets. The costs of improving realisation are minimal, usually requiring no additional staffing in most law firms. Every pound that a firm can recover is almost pure profit.

Poor realisation is not a matter of leaving money on the table – it is leaving money out in the street. The firm has earned that money already. It is theirs. All that it needs to do is retrieve it.

Realisation data also offers a reliable gateway to identifying and understanding some of the most important causes of poor profitability, which might have been unnoticed, perhaps almost invisible, for years. Most unrealised fees are the result of flaws in the firm, not obstinacy or bad faith on the part of clients.

There are three distinct realisation rates. Each one relates to a critical point in the work and billing cycle at which even an otherwise well-managed law firm can lose lots of money. Notwithstanding the thought experiment at the beginning of this section, no law firm can ever achieve and sustain 100% realisation; but better alertness to, and understanding of, the factors that influence realisation measurements at each of these critical points can produce dramatic improvements in overall profitability with only minimum effort and expense.

2.1 Recording realisation: what percentage of billable work is recorded?

It is easy to analyse data that is recorded, but how does one ascertain and evaluate facts that never appear on a timesheet or in a database? Recorded realisation is the most difficult to measure of the three types of realisation, but it also can be the most telling in its effects. The authors' efforts to estimate recording realisation rates, based on interviews primarily of law firm associates in small and midsize law

"Poor realisation is not a matter of leaving money on the table – it is leaving money out in the street. The firm has earned that money already. It is theirs. All that it needs to do is retrieve it."

firms, suggest that approximately 10% to 15% of the billable work they perform is never recorded. The most frequent reason stated is, "It took too long, and I assumed that the client would not pay for this work." The next most frequent reason, in a distant second place, is "I forgot".

The first reason, the assumption that the time would be written down or written off before billing, can be addressed easily through universal timekeeping. A law firm should insist that all fee earners – including partners, who are not immune to the tendency to second-guess whether a client will pay – record all potentially billable time, without regard to the fee structure (eg, hourly rate or fixed fee) or whether the time spent is within the reasonable expectations of the firm in constructing a non-hourly fee or of the client who has agreed to pay an hourly rate.

Forgetfulness, especially in the environment of a busy office, is harder to manage. When the authors have tried to measure the leakage resulting from forgetting to record time, based on self-reported estimates rather than observational measurements, it typically has been about 3% to 5% per day of delay. In other words, if a fee earner waits until the next day to record time, he or she is likely to underestimate it by a small, but nonetheless significant amount. Lawyers who work on many different files during a day tend to report the highest leakage rates if they did not record the time promptly. Those who work on only two or three matters during the day are usually more accurate even after several days, but still not perfect.

Forgetfulness and delay are a dangerous combination. The longer a fee earner waits to record billable work, the less accurate the recorded time will be. In most cases, tardy time recorders seem to err on the side of underestimating the time they spent.

The cumulative effect of tardy time recording

- An associate records an average of seven billable hours per day at a value of £150 per hour.[19] The associate typically works on four to six different files each day, but does not record time until the next day.
- Assuming a recording realisation leakage of only 3%, the unrealised time per day is 0.21 hours, with a value of £31.50 per day.
- If this not terribly forgetful associate works 200 days per year, the value of the forgotten time is £6,300.
- If there are a total of 12 associates in the firm, and each one has similar habits for recording work and similar accuracy of memory from one day to the next, the best case loss from unrecorded time could be £75,600. In some firms that is the equivalent of another associate's annual salary.

This model assumes consistent next-day recording habits across the firm. If associates wait until the end of the week to record their time, the effects of inaccurate recall are likely to increase, especially if a fee earner does not have any written notes or calendar notations. Small amounts of time might disappear entirely from memory and efforts to estimate the time spent on larger tasks might become little more than well-intentioned guesswork.

Improved time recording is the easiest way to improve overall realisation and profitability. A firm that bills hourly rates will never collect fees from hours that it doesn't record. A firm that bills on a fixed fee will never know the true amount of work needed to deliver a legal service within the fee budget. A strategy to improve overall realisation must therefore start with some clear, rigorously enforced standards for recording billable time:

- All potentially billable work should be recorded the same day that it is performed. The day's work is not done until all the time has been recorded and submitted.
- Associates and junior fee earners should not make assumptions about what work will or will not be paid for by the client.

2.2 Billing realisation: what percentage of the value of recorded work is billed?

This question bifurcates based on the fee structure of a matter. If a matter is billed as an hourly fee, the principal reason for writing off or reducing the time that is billed is usually an assumption that the client will not pay for that work. Curiously, this assumption is seldom tested by asking the client, such as by sending a proposed bill to the client for review before issuing the invoice.

The effects of weak billing realisation are subtler, but equally important, in matters with a non-hourly fee structure, such as a fixed fee. The recorded time will not normally appear on the bill, so if the number of hours is excessive, the client will usually never know. In fact, sometimes the partner supervising the matter will never know either. Nonetheless, the billing partner should use the same thought processes of reviewing the time recorded on a matter before sending a non-hourly bill to the client. In this instance, the question is not whether the client will pay, but whether the amount of time recorded for each task and service is consistent with the assumptions that the firm made when calculating the fixed fee. Just as an hour that must be written off before billing represents an hourly fee that the firm will never receive, an hour that is inconsistent with the assumptions underlying a fixed fee, and which must therefore be mentally written off, represents an hour's worth of overhead that produced no fee.

"The question is not whether the client will pay, but whether the amount of time recorded for each task and service is consistent with the assumptions that the firm made when calculating the fixed fee."

A second factor in low billing realisation is overdue unbilled work in progress in hourly rate matters. Depending on the agreed billing terms, clients are more likely to object to, and billing partners are more likely to find it difficult to explain billing delays in, unbilled work that is more than 60 days old. These hours frequently are written off when, had they been billed sooner, they would have been paid without objection. Billing partners often conclude, and the authors would tend to agree in most instances, that the collection of hourly fees arising from old work in progress is not worth the possible risk to a productive client relationship.

Regardless of the agreed billing schedule for a client or matter, billing partners should review time records every month for each matter under their cognisance. This is a very reliable way to detect issues with the amount of time that it is taking for fee earners, including partners working on the matter, to perform the necessary functions and tasks. It also is an excellent method for spotting problems with recording realisation. Beyond this basic requirement, firms should observe clear written policies and guidelines governing write-offs and write-downs by partners.

Write-offs and write-downs: suggested guidelines
- Only the billing partner may write off or write down recorded time. Everyone else working on the matter leaves that decision to the billing partner and records all time.
- Hours recorded for matters with non-hourly fees are subject to a formal write-off or adjustment, just as hourly rate billable hours are. Writing off time has significant implications for the profitability of a matter, regardless of the fee structure.
- Except for correcting obvious errors, the amount of work that a partner may write off or write down is limited, either in terms of the percentage of the total bill that the partner may adjust, or as a maximum value of the recorded time. This policy is especially important for work that is billed at an hourly rate.
- Major write-offs or write-downs may require the agreement of a second partner or approval by a practice group head or managing partner; and they are reported to the entire partnership. There are two important reasons for this practice:
- In hourly rate matters, a major write-off or write-down has a substantial immediate effect on revenue and profits.
- In non-hourly rate matters, the discovery of otherwise unbillable hours in a matter is an important indicator of an underlying problem, such as the efficiency or quality of the work being performed, the skills and knowledge of the fee earner who was assigned the task, or the validity of the assumptions on which the firm based its non-hourly fee.

These guidelines are not just important for ensuring consistency among partners. They also enable management to know exactly the amount of potential revenue being withdrawn from the invoice, the nature of the work involved, and the reasons for the action.

2.3 Collections realisation: what percentage of billed work is paid?
For firms that bill on an hourly basis, a collections realisation rate above 95% is considered excellent. This percentage can be raised to almost 100% by sending a pre-bill to the client and resolving any questions or disputes before the invoice is issued.

Even if a firm uses pre-bill reviews by clients to improve collections realisation, it should also routinely use other methods to improve the probability of full collection.

Other collections improvement methods
- Every partner should be responsible for monitoring the age of the work in progress and accounts receivable that he or she manages.
- The designated billing partner for a matter must be more than the person who approves the invoices. A billing partner should

have a sufficient working knowledge of the matter to be able to identify problems in the efficiency and timeliness with which all major functions in the matter, including administrative and financial ones, are being performed. This rule might be contrary to traditional practice in many law firms; but it is essential in the fast-moving practice environments of today's legal services industry, and more easily implemented with the support of the practice management systems that are now available even to the smallest law firms and solo practitioners.

- Prompt billing should be the individual responsibility of the billing partner, not the accounting department, practice group leader or managing partner.
- Likewise, the billing partner, not a clerk or bookkeeper, should carry the primary responsibility for prompt collections. The authors have observed that the most common characteristic of firms that keep collections realisation rates above 95% is that they have a culture of individual partner accountability.
- All partners should be required to monitor their unbilled work in progress and disbursements, with a proactive duty to notify the management of the firm when they increase beyond acceptable limits.
- One of the most useful methods for managing working capital, including work in progress and accounts receivable, is for all the partners in a small firm or a practice group to hold regular meetings to review all recorded but unbilled work and all accounts receivable under their cognisance. This is an excellent way to spot patterns and systemic issues in realisation rates that might not be as readily visible in individual matters.
- Work constantly to reduce the most frequent reasons for fee disputes. In this respect, time records are more than raw data for invoices. They also document how a firm or practice group works. Close attention to, and ongoing analysis of, time records over even as few as three or four months can lead to accurate insights about the most influential factors in fee disputes. Once identified and defined, these causes can usually be mitigated or eliminated altogether.

It is always better to eliminate the causes of expensive problems than constantly have to scurry to fix the problems after they arise.

3. Realisation as a diagnostic indicator

Realisation rates are some of the strongest diagnostic indicators of problems in law firm profitability, and they will become even more valuable as law firms attempt to remain competitive in disrupted legal markets. Of all the six classic drivers, realisation has the strongest link to sustainable profitability, because it measures the gap between the value of the work performed in terms of potential fees, and the revenue actually collected. Even a modest improvement in a realisation rate can produce disproportionately large improvements in profitability, not only for the short term but also going forward; and of all the measurements derived from the six classic drivers, realisation is one of the most responsive to market changes that affect long-term profitability. Disruptions often appear first as changes in the realisation data.

3.1 Diagnostic hypotheses arising from low billing realisation rates

If the billing realisation rate for a firm or practice group is declining, that often can be a sign of:

- inadequate knowledge or skills of fee earners;
- inadequate knowledge management systems, policies, or practices;
- unnecessarily time-consuming or inefficient internal processes in the preparation and delivery of a client service, especially in document-intensive services; or
- inadequate or unclear internal communication of the purpose, scope, or expectations concerning tasks performed by fee earners.

3.2 Diagnostic hypotheses arising from low collection realisation

Unsatisfactory collection realisation rates are usually indicators of:

- preventable errors in the billing process;
- weaknesses in the firm's policies or practices concerning timely billing and collections;
- client dissatisfaction with the results of the engagement;
- vulnerabilities in the firm's credit risk assessment practices when accepting a new client; or
- weak risk management practices to detect and respond promptly to changes in the client's financial position that might affect the ability to pay the firm's fees.

3.3 Variation in realisation rates as a diagnostic indicator

The primary goal of close observation of realisation rates is to try to nudge realisation up to as close to 100% as possible. Even a 1% increase can produce substantial additional profit. From the diagnostic perspective, it is more important to watch for variation, that is, significant discrepancies between short-term performance and long-range averages.

For example, if a practice group has steadily reported an 88% collection realisation over an extended period, and that rate suddenly drops to 75%, that change should receive attention. It is imperative to discover what factor or factors caused or influenced that deterioration in collection realisation. Likewise, if the collection rate suddenly increases from 88% to 96%, this might be a sign that the practice group is doing something better than before. The lawyers in the practice group need to find out what accounts for the improvement and to try to make it permanent.

Conditions warranting attention to realisation rate variations
- There is no apparent external explanation (or special cause) for the variation.
- The change in performance has continued for:
- at least three consecutive months; or
- three months during a period of five consecutive months.
- Wide variations from month to month suggest that realisation is out of control.

4. Better profits through better realisation
Any improvement in realisation produces almost pure profit. It does not require a collections crackdown against slow-paying clients. Instead, most of the keys to improved realisation can be found in the inner workings of the firm.

For example, instead of just saying, "We spent more time on this task than the client will accept as reasonable" and writing off or reducing a

"Of all the six classic drivers, realisation has the strongest link to sustainable profitability, because it measures the gap between the value of the work performed in terms of potential fees, and the revenue actually collected."

potential fee, the more productive use of realisation data is to use it to launch and guide an inquiry into the nature of the work and the factors that can contribute to it taking longer than expected. Addressing these issues usually costs only a tiny fraction of the amount that the client refuses to pay. Moreover, paying attention to each of the three types of realisation can lead to greater sustainable improvements in profitability than any of the other six classic drivers.

What would another 10%, or even only another 5%, in fee revenue add to your firm's profitability? What would it mean to be able to achieve that increase at little or no additional cost, almost as pure profit? For most law firms that money, which has already been earned, is waiting to be picked up through better management of realisation.

Cost management – classic driver #4

1. A thought experiment: operating a law firm for £50 per hour
You are the operations manager of a 50-person general practice firm in a medium-sized city. The firm consists of:

- 10 equity partners;
- 20 associates; and
- 20 full-time support staff.

The total fee revenue for the last fiscal year was slightly more than £6 million, and has remained at that level, plus or minus £200,000, for the past three years. The FLOC last year, which excludes partner compensation, was £2.8 million, producing an average profit per equity partner of £220,000. It is now the end of the fiscal year, and the partners realise that this year's performance will be similarly disappointing. They have directed you to develop a business plan that will improve profitability.

"We all understand the value of long-term sustainable profitability," the senior partner explains to you, "but we need to get the biggest possible gain right away. Unless we start showing a dramatic increase in profits immediately, we will start to lose some of our partners, some of whom are earning less than associates in some of the other firms in town."

The senior partner says that the partners have examined their individual books of business to find growth opportunities, but do not expect to produce substantially more fee revenue in a legal market that has recently been disrupted by predatory pricing and the incursion of non-traditional providers of legal services who offer many of the same services that your firm delivers, but at a significantly lower price.

"The other partners and I feel that the only opportunity to recover profitability is to cut costs," the senior partner concludes. "We want you to come up with a plan to cut our operating costs to approximately £50 per lawyer hour."

You begin to protest, but the senior partner waves her hand and interrupts. "Yes, I know," she says. "We're talking about short-term gratification at the possible expense of long-term results. I would like to see permanent cost reductions and sustainable profitability, if possible, but I don't think it can be done."

Over the past three years the FLOC per lawyer hour has risen slightly from £113 to £119. How are you going to cut costs by more than 50% and sustain them at that level? Where will you look for that magnitude of cost reductions?

2. Cost management in context

None of the first three of the six classic drivers discussed in this report are fast and easy ways to improve the profitability of a law firm or practice group:

- It is no longer reasonable to build a profitability strategy on *increased prices* – price resistance has emerged as one of the most prominent features of the disrupted legal market.
- *Productivity* promises powerful increases in fee revenue, even as the acceptable prices for legal services continue to drop or, at best, remain stagnant; but the promise of exponentially improved productivity relies on the adoption and management of new legal practice technology, including artificial intelligence, that is still in its infancy and which, when mature, will require the mastery of fundamentally new ways of producing and delivering legal services.
- The diagnostic benefits of closer management of *realisation* can form the foundations of sustainable improvements in profitability at relatively low cost, but attaining them requires a degree of management discipline and, in some instances, cultural change that many traditional law firms continue to resist.

3. The temptation to slash costs

The scenario described in the thought experiment above replicates the traditional first reaction of many leaders and managers of law firms that are suffering from stagnating profitability: cut costs to carve more profit from the revenue that the firm already has. Such dramatic cost-cutting crusades frequently emerge as a firm approaches the third quarter of its fiscal year, as a quick way to improve profitability and increase the year-end distributions to partners. The cost-cutting hawks point out that some cost savings can be accomplished overnight, while most revenue increases take months to develop, if they are available at all. Moreover, the most attractive opportunities to save money are usually already present within the firm, and can be implemented without alienating clients with potentially futile efforts to nudge fees upwards, or annoying fee earners by demanding that they bill more hours and collect more bills.

Although this approach might appear to be short-sighted, quick cost cutting is possible. Law firms today have an increasing variety of options for the management of their internal operations, ranging from technology support, to facilities management, to personnel management and payroll. These innovative approaches to running a law practice have extended to new models for the preparation and

"The cost-cutting hawks point out that some cost savings can be accomplished overnight, while most revenue increases take months to develop, if they are available at all."

delivery of the legal services themselves. All of these have the potential to reduce costs. To this extent, the disruption of the operational aspects of the legal services industry appears to be positive.

At the same time, poorly thought-out cost management, even when it produces quick positive results, can make things much worse in the long term. There are almost infinite ways to mismanage costs in a law firm; but five common mistakes seem to be particularly dangerous and to have the most serious long-term consequences, especially for smaller law firms and solo practices, both of which have little tolerance for blunders in financial management.

Each of these cost-management pitfalls has a direct impact on profitability by imposing measurable costs, sometimes opportunity costs, that can pull financial performance down. The best cost-management strategy is a blend of audacious exploitation of clever innovation inside the firm and cautious avoidance of these pitfalls of cost management.

4. Pitfall number 1: not knowing what it costs to produce a legal service

This report has already introduced the concept of fully loaded operating cost (FLOC) per lawyer hour as one of the most important but underused financial measurements available to a law firm. What is the true cost of the production of a legal product or service?

Fully loaded operating cost is a simple concept; but a surprising number of small and midsize law firms have never heard of it. Rather than invest the modest amount of time and analysis needed to develop a fully textured understanding of what it costs to produce a legal service, they use guesswork and wishful thinking to propose a fee that they hope will be competitive and profitable. This is the leading reason why law firms lose money on fixed fee work and slash hourly rates to unprofitable levels in hopes of remaining competitive in a disrupted legal market.

FLOC is the total operating cost of the law firm for one year. In addition to basic costs such as facilities, equipment and supplies, it includes salaries and benefits for staff and lawyers who are not equity partners. Fully loaded operating costs do not include purchases and investments paid from the capital of the firm or financed externally. There are several ways that law firms typically define FLOC:

4.1 Firm-wide FLOC
The firm's FLOC is allocated equally on a per-lawyer or per-fee-earner basis.

"Fully loaded operating cost is a simple concept; but a surprising number of small and midsize law firms have never heard of it."

For example, a firm has a FLOC of approximately £21 million and 80 full-time lawyers. The FLOC per lawyer would be £262,500 (£21 million divided by 80 full-time lawyers).

4.2 Practice group FLOC

Firms that have practice group or practice department budgets sometimes allocate FLOC based on the actual operating budget of the practice group. FLOC under this model includes these components:

- any shared costs that are allocated on a firm-wide basis (such as utilities, premises insurance, information technology services, library and research services, firm marketing, and firm-wide shared services);
- personnel costs that are attributable exclusively to the practice group (such as staff and non-partner salaries and benefits); and
- marketing and other costs specific to the practice group.

Using the same firm described in the previous example, assume that the litigation practice group consists of:

- two equity partners;
- six other lawyers; and
- eight support staff, some of whom perform paralegal duties.

666666

The elements of the practice group's FLOC include the following:

- The firm has a shared FLOC (not including salaries and personnel benefits) of £83,000 per lawyer, consisting of expenses and shared services that are allocated on a per-capita basis firm-wide.
- The practice group has 14 non-partner staff (administrative, paralegal and non-partner lawyers) with a total compensation and benefits budget of £1.3 million.
- The litigation practice group also has a separate marketing budget of £50,000 per year.

Table 1: Litigation practice group FLOC

Firm-wide FLOC allocated to the litigation practice group (£83,000 per lawyer multiplied by 8 lawyers)	£664,000
Compensation for non-partner lawyers, paralegals and staff in the litigation practice group	£1,300,000
Litigation practice group marketing budget	£50,000
Total FLOC for the litigation practice group	£2,014,000
FLOC per lawyer in the litigation practice group (£2,014,000 divided by 8)	£251,750

Note that FLOC per lawyer in the litigation practice group is less than the £262,500 FLOC per lawyer firm-wide. Assuming that the firm's litigation practice can produce an average fee yield per lawyer hour that is comparable to or better than the firm-wide average, this suggests that the litigation group might be somewhat more profitable than the firm as a whole.

Assuming that the eight lawyers in the group recorded a total of 14,000 billable hours per year, this would produce a FLOC per lawyer hour of £143.86. To be marginally profitable (14 pence per hour!) at 100% realisation, a lawyer in the litigation group would have to produce an average fee yield of at least £144 per hour. Viewing this calculation from a cost-management perspective, the litigation group must be able to manage its FLOC at or below £143.86 per hour.

The main point of this exercise, however, is to illustrate that unless the litigation practice group is aware of its own FLOC – and not just that of the entire firm – it cannot be confident that it is managing its costs within its fee expectations, nor that the fees that it agrees, whether hourly or non-hourly, will produce a reasonable profit for the firm.

4.3 FLOC per fee earner

In firms or practice groups that have a significant number of paralegal or other non-lawyer fee earners, it is sometimes more accurate to include non-lawyer fee earners in the calculation in order to generate a FLOC per fee earner. This variant can be especially useful when these four conditions exist:

- Non-lawyer fee earners typically contribute at least 40% of their time to the same or similar matters. This assures a reasonable level of familiarity with, and consistency in the performance of, the tasks assigned to the non-lawyer fee earner.
- Each non-lawyer fee earner who participates in the matter typically spends at least 40% of his or her time performing billable work.
- The firm or practice group has frequent and substantial experience delegating billable work to non-lawyers. Poor delegation techniques and inadequate management of delegated work are the two leading causes of write-offs of otherwise billable hours recorded by non-lawyers.
- The firm or practice group has functioning, documented, and consistently applied quality assurance policies and procedures to avoid unnecessary inefficiencies and errors in the delegated work. In some firms that the authors have observed, as much as 70% of the write-offs of non-lawyer work is attributable to rework to correct errors that could have been avoided through better quality assurance.

5. Pitfall number 2: overinvestment in multiple offices

In the era of globalisation of legal services, there is a temptation for law firms to expand geographically. Small local firms see new competitors enter their communities from elsewhere; and they wonder whether their own geographic expansion will help them to open new fields from which to harvest new clients.

Multiple offices can nudge upward a wide range of items in fully loaded cost, such as support staff requirements and equipment. It is not unusual, therefore, to find branch offices that are underutilised – often empty for a large part of the week – and do not produce enough revenue to cover their expenses. The authors also have observed that, with some very well-managed exceptions, the FLOC per lawyer in multiple-office firms usually is at least 10% higher than in single-office firms. This premium can be even higher in some high-cost locations like New York, London and Hong Kong.

What is the business case for opening a new office? This needs to include realistic projections of additional fee revenues, ideally based on expressions of interest and support by existing clients with operations in the new location under consideration. The old aspiration

"One of the new realities of the disrupted legal market is that clients rely more – and in many instances exclusively – on electronic lawyer–client relationships and interactions, no longer expecting or perceiving significant value in face-to-face meetings in the lawyer's office."

– "If we open an office, the clients will come" – rarely comes true. One of the new realities of the disrupted legal market is that clients rely more – and in many instances exclusively – on electronic lawyer–client relationships and interactions, no longer expecting or perceiving significant value in face-to-face meetings in the lawyer's office. Even if there is a strong business case to open a new office elsewhere, before investing in full-time staff and a long-term lease in a new location, most law firms should look at starting with a virtual office or serviced space in a business centre. This will allow the firm to minimise its losses if the new office fails to meet its financial expectations.

6. Pitfall number 3: not keeping up with the technology

The economics of law firm technology continue to change quickly and dramatically; but many firms are a decade behind in how they manage technology costs.

Leasing computer equipment and software is now less expensive for most small and midsize firms than purchasing it. Even if a firm prefers to own its equipment, the partners must resist the temptation to shave costs by postponing upgrades and replacements. This is a false economy, which in a fast-moving technology environment no longer provides even short-term financial relief. When computers start to break down and software begins to fail, the overall costs in lost productivity and higher unplanned replacement costs almost always surpass the short-term savings.

The even bigger danger is that of falling so far behind the competition that it quickly becomes prohibitively expensive to catch up. As with almost every other information technology service, product, technology, or system, the cost of law practice technology continues to drop. Outsourced, internet-based services, including artificially intelligent systems, are moving into the range of affordability – and, the authors would argue, necessity – for even small firms and some solo practitioners. Their return on investment in terms of exponentially increased productivity is already compelling, especially for firms that deliver high-volume services involving relatively standardised tasks in a price-sensitive disrupted legal market.

7. Pitfall number 4: ignoring partner performance issues

Few law firms can afford the cost of carrying an unproductive partner at a high level of remuneration for very long. At the same time, many law firm partnerships dread the prospect of having to impose sanctions such as a reduction in compensation or profit shares, forced buy-out of an equity partner, or asking the partner to leave the firm. Instead, half-hoping that things will get better on their own, these firms often wait to take any action, other than perhaps a few indirect gentle admonitions, until a partner's financial performance has become a profitability crisis. In smaller firms, especially, one or two unproductive partners can pull an entire practice group from profit down into chronic losses.

Confronting substandard partner performance is, above all, a cost-management issue. It seldom is comfortable, especially if the partner is an older, well-respected lawyer whose performance has declined with age. In many cases, counselling, coaching, and a resetting of the partner's goals and responsibilities can help the partner to return to making a profitable contribution to the firm. This requires skilled outside assistance and facilitation. Well-intentioned efforts to save money with a do-it-yourself intervention never helps and almost always makes it worse.

There is no cheap solution to the problem of declining partner performance; but the most expensive approach is to do nothing at all.

8. Pitfall number 5: slashing costs without managing risks
This could be the costliest cost-management pitfall of all. It can produce nightmares, not visions, with unintended consequences that can seriously hurt and possibly destroy a law firm's reputation and its ability to continue to compete successfully in a disrupted market.

"There is no cheap solution to the problem of declining partner performance; but the most expensive approach is to do nothing at all."

It is especially ironic in this era of rapid change and intense competition in the legal services industry that law firms can develop well-informed, carefully thought-out business plans to manage their expansion efforts; but few of them apply the same imagination, insight, intellectual rigour, and business prudence to cost reductions.

Case study: the consequences of slashing costs

A 90-lawyer law firm decided to boost year-end profits by more than £1.2 million by firing 30 paralegal and clerical staff members. Most of these worked in the firm's high-volume collections and trademarks registration practices. The firm's 20 partners were delighted to pocket an extra £60,000 each, even the two who supervised the collections and trademarks departments.

The staff cutbacks created a minor avalanche in the firm. Three more senior staff left the collections and trademarks practice within the first four months of the new fiscal year. The HR director attempted to conduct exit interviews with the three people as they departed. One of the departing staff members said that the recent staff reductions "were a clear sign to me that this ship is sinking". The second member complained about having to take on the extra work left behind by the people who were terminated at what was referred to by the firm's employees as the "December Massacre". The third senior staff member declined to be interviewed. These three senior staff were essential and had to be replaced, with overtime, temporary staffing, and replacement costs totalling more than £60,000. This was an unexpected and unbudgeted cost.

The collections and trademarks departments tried to work more efficiently with fewer staff. The overworked survivors had to work faster and longer, as they struggled to handle the work left behind by their fired co-workers. Despite these efforts, processing times for client matters and response times to client inquiries began to grow steadily. The two practices also experienced an average increase of 20% in recorded time arising from the need to correct an increasing number of errors. Of course, this rework could not be billed, as the clients would have justifiably refused to pay for it.

Clients began to notice that something was wrong. Client dissatisfaction and fee disputes began to increase sharply approximately four months after the cutbacks. By the end of the fiscal year, the firm had lost almost £2 million in potential fees, about half of which represented new matters for which existing clients instructed other law firms which, as one client put it, "I can be more confident will meet my needs and expectations". Fee disputes had increased the average fee payment time for the two departments from 58 days to 147 days.

The staff cutbacks had other impacts. Absenteeism increased in the two departments, resulting in more than £20,000 in overtime and another £20,000 in temporary staffing costs in the first year alone. These costs were unplanned and unbudgeted.

The firm "saved" £1.2 million, but its failure to anticipate and manage the risks of its cost-cutting scheme cost the firm more than £2.1 million, for a net loss of more than £900,000. This did not include the intangible negative value of the long-term damage to the firm's reputation among collections and trademarks clients, declining staff morale, and potential losses due to unresolved fee disputes.

8.1 Resisting the temptation to slash and burn

Dramatic cost reductions get attention and can produce significant short-term improvements in profitability that put more money into the partners' pockets. However, as the above case study shows, these gains can be obliterated by failure to anticipate the long-term consequences. Moreover, a law firm might end up in a worse position financially than had the cost cuts never been attempted.

Although not nearly as adrenalin-producing, a careful analysis of the benefits and long-term impacts can lead to subtle, but potentially more rewarding, opportunities to improve profits. Even in what appears to be a dire financial emergency, this is usually the wiser course.

Staff compensation – classic driver #5

1. A thought experiment: associate compensation in 2030?
What will be your firm's total cost of associate compensation and benefits in 2030? What, if any, factors can you manage in order to keep that total cost at current levels, without affecting revenue production or the quality of your firm's legal services?

2. Are associates becoming inherently unprofitable?
The pay and benefits for salaried professionals is the largest item in most law firms' operating budgets, typically consuming between 40% and 60% of a firm's total revenue. In traditional law firms, as in most businesses, one of the most cost-effective ways to improve profitability was to improve productivity by hiring more associates. This approach improved leverage, as discussed in the next section of this report, by delegating legal work to lower-paid but competent lawyers, thereby freeing partners to concentrate their efforts on higher-priced services and business development.

Beginning in the mid-1990s, however, and, with a brief pause during the recession of 2008–10, steadily increasing salary expectations have produced disappointing results for many law firms. They find themselves being forced, they believe, to pay ever-increasing salaries to attract and retain the best associates; but the partners do not perceive an equivalent return on their investment in terms of proportionately high profit distributions. As a partner in a US firm said, "For every dollar we pay in higher associate salaries, we are lucky if we realise 50 cents in increased fee revenues and even less in terms of additional profits."

This partner's casual observation might overstate the case a little, but the underlying trend has been towards ever-increasing salaries, even for inexperienced first-year associates. As associates remain in a firm, they naturally expect raises commensurate with their experience. However, in many of the legal markets in which these well-paid associates practice, clients are reluctant to pay commensurately higher fees. As a result, it has become a common phenomenon after five or six years to see the net income produced by an associate start to level off, and the return on the investment in the associate's salary begin to decrease.

It is not surprising, therefore, that associate compensation often has been the most poorly managed element of law firm profitability. Moreover, changes in the nature of law firm work, which are already underway, could make associate compensation an even greater obstacle to profitability. Little wonder, then, that in some firms partners have simply given up. They expect that associates' financial

"Most law firms will need substantially fewer associates in 2030 than they have now. In fact, some might no longer need traditional associates at all."

expectations will continue to rise, and that partners' expectations should diminish as profit distributions grow more slowly or even stagnate, due in large part to a squeeze between a downward press on fee tolerances in most legal markets and an ever-increasing upward pressure for high associate compensation.

The authors agree with the first half of this grim scenario but disagree with the second. The entry of young, highly talented associates into the legal services industry is disrupting many of the traditional ways in which law firms operated; but these changes do not have to be at the expense of sustainable profitability.

3. Looking through the wrong end of the telescope

This sense of resignation to ever-increasing staff compensation, especially for associates, and a related stagnation or decline in profitability overlooks two important factors that are only now emerging in the legal services industry, but which will continue to influence and reshape the role of staff compensation in law firm profitability for the foreseeable future.

The first factor is that much of the attention and commentary about associate compensation focuses on the individual salaries that law firms believe they must pay in order to recruit and retain the best lawyers. However, as discussed in more detail in the next section of this report, most law firms can expect to see their staffing requirements for associates decrease sharply over the next 10 years. As technology enables associates to become 10, 12, or even 20 times more productive with respect to certain routine and currently time-consuming tasks, the number of associates that a law firm will need to perform traditional associate work, especially in a disrupted technology-driven legal services industry, will decrease dramatically. This decline in associate staffing requirements will be further accelerated as artificially intelligent systems take over the document review, analysis, and drafting functions currently performed by human lawyers.

Most law firms will need substantially fewer associates in 2030 than they have now. In fact, some might no longer need traditional associates at all. Those associates that do remain will need to have advanced skills in information management and the operation of legal technology systems. A title such as 'legal services technician' might be more appropriate than 'associate'; and this new type of law firm associate will undoubtedly command a higher salary than even some of the best-paid traditional associates today. However, the overall compensation costs for associates in a law firm, as well as the ratio of compensation costs to the value of their work output, will be much lower.

The second factor, as pointed out later in this section, is that associate profitability is a partner problem, arising from inadequate management and not from a lack of motivation or a weak work ethic. Even if there is not much that most law firms can do about rising associate compensation, they can ensure that they have managed associates to a point of maximum profitability. Having strong, flexible associate management policies and systems in place now will, more than any other management strategy or innovation, assure the most cost-effective transition when technology begins to perform substantially more of the tasks and functions handled by associates today.

4. It's not about the money

Over the past 20 years, the authors have conducted focus groups, interviews and informal discussions on the subject of career expectations with more than 1,000 associates in law firms throughout the world. Their message is consistent: Compensation is not the most important reason they accept employment or decide to remain at their respective law firms. In some groups, even those from firms that did not pay above-median salaries for their respective markets, pay was not even mentioned. Instead, three other factors have always appeared at the top of the focus groups' lists, although not necessarily always in the same order.

Considerations when accepting employment
- **Professional development:** Associates have consistently told the authors that one of the most important factors is the opportunity to obtain practical legal skills and to develop them through experience. They expect more responsibility and greater professional and intellectual experiences as they build experience with the firm. The prospect of merely grinding out billable work, day in and day out for five, six, or seven years is unattractive, notwithstanding the pay that they might earn for working so hard.
- **Mentoring:** The associates in the authors' focus groups want a close professional relationship with a partner or other senior lawyer from whom they can learn the profession. They are frequently disappointed by law firms that pay only lip service to mentoring or, even more frustrating, allow partners to take highly inconsistent approaches to their mentoring responsibilities, ranging from insightful ongoing guidance and support to total indifference.
- **Career paths and options:** Associates want to know what they must do to succeed in their respective firms. Is it possible to have a successful career without assuming the financial responsibilities of equity partnership in, or other ownership of, the firm? Young lawyers are attracted to firms offering a career

plan that documents the requirements, options, and guidance needed for a young lawyer to manage advancement in the firm. They also value having realistic performance goals by which they can measure their progress.

These three factors are so strong that most of the associates in the authors' focus groups would consider accepting a lower salary than they could earn at another firm, provided that the firm delivers better professional development and career management opportunities, and a more supportive work environment.

Aspirations eventually collide with financial realities, however. When associates' salaries drop below the median in the market for lawyers with similar credentials and experience, those associates are at serious risk of being recruited away from the firm, despite the attractive non-monetary benefits that they might have to give up.

5. Improving associate profitability now

In most firms that have associate profitability problems, the root cause is not that associates are overpaid. This is like blaming the existence of the kilogram for obesity. Instead, those associates might be under-managed. Most law firms, even ones with relatively sophisticated

"The carrot and stick philosophy of motivation seldom works in law firms. Many lawyers, even associates, dislike carrots and have long ago learned not to fear the stick."

"Like any other strategic asset, associates must be viewed as an investment, not a liability; and partners should be able to expect a consistently positive return on that investment if it is well managed."

management policies and practices in other areas, do not measure the total economic contribution and profitability of each associate. Their associates may or may not be overpaid, but they are certainly under-managed.

Measuring associate profitability using the metrics suggested throughout this report is the first step towards improving it. The measurements should be used as diagnostic tools to identify issues and improvements, and not as a whip to terrorise associates into working harder. The carrot and stick philosophy of motivation seldom works in law firms. Many lawyers, even associates, dislike carrots and have long ago learned not to fear the stick.

Low profitability is usually caused by incomplete skills or inconsistent professional supervision, not a poor work ethic or, more recently, the "Millennials are different" excuse. Productivity issues likewise frequently can be traced back to an inadequate investment by partners in the professional development of their associates. When weaknesses in professional skills or knowledge is found in one associate, there is a high probability that other associates in the practice group, or even throughout the entire firm, have similar problems.

The second step in better financial management of associates is to have agreed performance goals. In many firms, the only goal that an associate has is, as one associate in a British law firm said, "Do the work my partner gives to me, as best as I can." By contrast, law firms that manage associate profitability regularly measure their performance against a set of individual goals, where each goal is:

- specific;
- measurable;
- agreed;
- realistic;
- time-related; and
- ultimately linked to the firm's business plan.

To be meaningful, performance goals must be supported by ongoing feedback by a partner or senior lawyer, along with formal periodic evaluation and incentives. For this reason, firms that have a strong system of performance goals also have partners who regard mentoring and professional development as one of their most important duties.

6. Money into the bottomless pit
Some law firm partners sometimes feel that associate compensation is a bottomless pit into which they must constantly throw money.

If traditional law firms hope to survive the disruption of the legal services industry that is already underway and is likely to continue indefinitely, they will need to do more than continue to throw money at associate profitability problems. Instead, some law firms will have to radically revise their thinking. Instead of being a draining cost centre, each associate in a law firm should be a profit centre, earning more in fees than he or she consumes in salary and support costs.

Like any other strategic asset, associates must be viewed as an investment, not a liability; and partners should be able to expect a consistently positive return on that investment if it is well managed. Like all investments, the effective management of associate compensation, as well as that of other personnel, demands ongoing attention to measurable performance, a diagnostic approach to performance measurement that leads to prompt inquiry when potential issues are spotted, and ongoing nurturing of the investment through better mentoring and professional development.

For these reasons, the authors recommend that law firms should integrate associate compensation, professional development, and career advancement into a single performance management system; one that links compensation and advancement to the performance standards that demonstrate an associate is acquiring and using the expertise and skills that he or she will need eventually to become a successful partner.

The long-term prognosis for associate compensation as one of the six classic drivers of profitability is optimistic. Every trend in the legal services industry today suggests that, over the next 10 years, associate compensation will decline as an inhibitor of associate profitability, as technology reduces the number of associates that most law firms will need, while greatly increasing the productivity of the associates that remain. A law firm does not have to wait 10 years, however, to improve the profitability of its associates and other staff. Better management, not just more money, can improve associate performance now, while law firms wait and watch for the impact of advanced technology and artificial intelligence to introduce fundamental changes in the generations-old model of how law firms work.

Leverage – classic driver #6

Give me a lever and a place to stand and I will move the Earth.
Archimedes of Syracuse (287–c 211 BCE)

1. A thought experiment: 40-to-1 leverage?

For many years, your firm has maintained a steady average ratio of four associates to one partner. This configuration has proven to be highly profitable, especially because you are a master of the art of delegation. By being required to supervise only four associates, you believe that you have a better opportunity to manage the quality of their work and mentor each one than one of your partners who has six associates working for her. You do not feel as chronically overworked as another of your partners who is supported by only two associates. Your firm's chief financial officer says that because you leverage your book of business so effectively, yours is one of the most profitable practices in the firm.

Your firm is investing in new law practice technology and is even beginning to introduce artificial intelligence into some analytical and drafting functions that previously were performed by associates and, in a few instances, by yourself. The consultants who are advising your firm tell you that within the next three years, you can expect each associate's productivity to increase at least 10 times. In other words, one associate will soon be producing the work that requires 10 associates today. Your comfortably profitable 4-to-1 leverage will quickly become, in effect, 40-to-1 by today's standards.

Suddenly, the prospect of your four associates producing the work of 40, if measured by today's work capacities, no longer seems to be such a good idea.

What changes will you need to make?

2. Finding the fulcrum

A well-leveraged law practice, even a small one, can indeed move a lawyer's whole world. Leverage explains why some small and midsize law firms can produce average profits per partner that are much higher than those of some of their larger, better-resourced competitors.

Despite its potential as one of the most powerful of the six classic drivers, leverage is frequently overlooked and underused. Most law firm partners intellectually understand the basic concept of leverage; but many do not know how to manage it well, unable to master the relationship between lever and fulcrum.

A partner's time is the fulcrum that gives leverage its great force; however, many law firm partnerships have never developed even a rough consensus about what is the best use of a partner's time and, as a result, how best to use associates. The authors continually observe two problems in the context of leverage:

- Most firms tend to treat leverage somewhat superficially, without the analytical depth and intellectual rigour required to produce the significant results that are possible in the profitable delivery of legal services. The focus is almost exclusively on the weaker of the two forms available – *staffing* leverage – at the expense of the more important *workflow* leverage.
- Technology- and client-driven disruptive forces in the legal market and the legal services industry are turning traditional concepts of leverage upside down and inside out. This is discussed in section 3 below.

2.1 Staffing leverage
What is the ratio of associates to partners?

There are a variety of nuanced options that are possible in this calculation. For example, some firms include recent law school graduates who have not yet qualified as lawyers in the associate category. This is usually a mistake, because in most law firms recent graduates and trainees do not perform the same functions, and at the same level of responsibility, as associates. Moreover, a substantial amount of their time might be consumed by performing what are essentially paralegal or clerical tasks. For these reasons, including recent graduates or trainees in the staffing leverage calculation can create a somewhat misleading impression of a higher functioning level of leverage than actually exists.

Likewise, some firms include of counsel lawyers or other senior post-associate, non-partner, positions in the "partner" constituency for purposes of calculating staffing leverage. This might produce a misleading impression of lower staffing leverage, because in many law firms the working and supervisory relationships between of counsel members of the firm and associates is not as extensive or consistent as those between partners and associates.

For purposes of calculating staffing leverage, some firms include as associates recent law graduates who have not yet qualified or been licensed to practice.

What is the "magic" ratio for staffing leverage? The thought experiment at the beginning of this section might suggest that a 4-to-1 ratio of associate to partner is generally considered to be profitable in most law firms. That might be the case for the firm in the thought experiment; but in real life the prevailing staffing leverage can vary according to factors such as firm size, practice specialty and region.

Law firm leverage varies widely by region and practice specialty. For example, it is not unusual to find Latin American firms with overall staffing leverages of 5-to-1 or 6-to-1. In fast-growing legal markets, like those in Latin America and Asia, most of the growth in law firm size takes place at associate level, while the number of partners tends to grow more slowly. In some cases this disparity in growth is due to the need to manage the financial, administrative and practice management transition from a firm's founding partners to the next generation.

Staffing leverage has also traditionally varied widely by practice area. High-volume practices such as intellectual property and some litigation specialties are more highly leveraged, with staffing leverage sometimes exceeding 6-to-1. However, as technology becomes more prominent in the preparation and delivery of legal services in such practice areas, the staffing leverage ratio is becoming somewhat more complex as technology-equipped non-lawyers take over functions formerly performed by associates.

Staffing leverage also is becoming more complex – but, the authors would suggest, less relevant – as some functions traditionally performed by associates inside a law firm are now being "leveraged"

"When advanced technology and artificially intelligent systems are applied to the work that associates perform, hiring more lawyers, even with delegation, could worsen profitability almost exponentially."

out of the firm completely through outsourcing to low-cost, high-volume legal services contractors. Whereas a high staffing ratio used to be a potential indicator – subject to further inspection, of course – of the profitable management of work inside a law firm, the growing availability and financial attractiveness of outsourcing might suggest that a high staffing ratio is becoming, instead, an indicator of missed opportunities to manage the work more profitably.

Staffing leverage is one part of the leverage driver, but it is only the starting point. Some law firms still cling to or pursue higher staffing leverage as a cure to their profitability problems. They assume that they need only hire more associates; and if that action does not solve the profitability problems, which it usually will not, these firms simply assume that they hired the wrong people and try again.

Hiring more associates will obviously improve the staffing leverage, but it does not improve profitability unless partners delegate more of their work to their new associates. In fact, simply hiring more lawyers without improving delegation usually worsens profitability. When advanced technology and artificially intelligent systems are applied to the work that associates perform, hiring more lawyers, even with delegation, could worsen profitability almost exponentially.

Instead, it is important to remember that staffing leverage is essentially an intellectual construct that helps to define the potential for improved profitability. It has no life or vitality of its own, and it contributes little to a well-informed understanding of how to improve the profitability of law firm operations. This deeper level of analysis – which the authors contend is the level that will truly matter in a disrupted legal services industry – requires an understanding of how the work actually gets done in a law firm's practice groups.

2.2 Workflow leverage

Walk through the corridors of any law firm in the world, and one is likely to see or hear these indicators of weak workflow leverage:

- By six o'clock in the evening all the associates have gone home; but the partners are still working in their offices at eight or later.
- Partners bill an average of 2,000 hours per year; but the average recorded billable hours for associates is 1,700 hours or less.
- Associates complain that they do not have enough work.

The principal advantage of workflow leverage is that it measures the actual amount of work that partners delegate to non-partners, whether associates, trainees, or other non-lawyer fee earners. The workflow leverage ratio that results from this calculation can be, and usually is, substantially less than the staffing ratio.

Until now, the authors have considered a workflow leverage of 5-to-1 as strong, and presumably very profitable, in most practice areas. In other words, the non-partner fee earners in a practice group, or in a team working with a partner on a particular matter, record five times the number of hours recorded by a partner. Higher volume practices often have even higher workflow leverage of 8-to-1 or 9-to-1, especially in practice areas that rely heavily on non-lawyer fee earners to perform functions that, in other firms, might be performed by associates.

Another advantage of using workflow rather than staffing leverage to assess the profitability of how the work is done is that it does not have to be limited to work performed in-house, but can include outsourced work too. This is becoming increasingly important as law firms begin to transform from essentially a 19th-century staffing model to an enterprise that creatively integrates, assembles and delivers legal services from components that are produced both inside and outside the traditional four walls of the firm. Workflow leverage can produce insights into this new model for the production of legal services that staffing ratios cannot begin to reach.

Before technology and artificial intelligence make any further, deeper incursions into how law firms function, it is very important that those firms master the concept of workflow leverage.

3. Technology, workflow leverage and the future of the law firm

Artificial intelligence systems will soon have the potential to boost workflow leverage in law firms at least tenfold and, in some practice specialties, up to one hundredfold and perhaps even higher. Consider the implications. They are almost mind-numbing.

If a law firm can perform legal analysis or documentation that used to take 10 hours of billable associate work in only 90 seconds, that will certainly reduce the cost of the service, even after including the investment in and ongoing maintenance of the technology; but will client awareness of these new capabilities create further downward pressure on fees?

Could the 40-to-1 workflow leverage hypothesised in the thought experiment at the beginning of this section – with four associates delivering 10 times the work for one partner to manage – make large law firms, with hundreds or thousands of lawyers, too unprofitable to survive? What will happen when one associate, for example, can produce in one hour the work product that currently takes 10 hours? This could have a dramatic impact on the need for associates in most law firms, and might even render the traditional partner and associate structure obsolete.

Some firms are still languishing in denial or attempts to differentiate themselves out of such scenarios. Still others believe that these are still somewhat academic questions, which can be deferred for at least a few more years. Only a very few law firms have begun to factor these likely developments into their strategic thinking. Even fewer are including the consequences for associate staffing levels in their preparations for the hyper-leveraged legal services industry that is already beginning to appear.

These are scary questions. As an initial response, the legal services industry needs to develop and begin to monitor a new definition of workflow leverage: the ratio of hours of billable work performed primarily by humans and the hour-equivalents produced primarily by artificial intelligence. Currently, such an AI leverage ratio would be relatively weak in most law firms, with the great majority of work still being performed by lawyers using traditional information management tools. However, sometime between 2025 and 2030, the legal services industry should expect to see the leverage ratio shift towards AI hour-equivalents. The tipping point will be different for each firm, but all firms will need to be ready to respond.

Being
the change

You must be the change that you want to see in the world.
Mohandas K Gandhi (1869–1948)

1. Introduction

Understanding and using the fundamentals of profitability, while grounded in intellectual realism, is not as straightforward as one might think. During their reconstruction and re-emergence after World War II as one of the world's top economic powers, the Japanese, buoyed by their work with W Edwards Deming,[20] recognised that how they got the work done was even more important than what they did. As discussed previously in this report, understanding how legal services are produced and delivered in a traditional law firm, and how that is already changing, will be the key to sustaining the profitability of those firms as they navigate through disrupted legal markets.

Law firm leaders are learning – often by trial and error – that to achieve their evolving goals, they need to document how to get them done. To develop and implement these written action plans for their strategic and business priorities, they need to communicate and work together in more collaborative ways. This internal and external collaboration, and its resulting innovation, leads to a continuous flow of new information, viewpoints and opportunity throughout a fiscal year and beyond.

2. Change-challenged or change-ready?

Legal markets worldwide are undergoing dramatic changes. Traditional law firms that are alert and nimble are the ones that are most likely to survive, as successful business and professional institutions did in the years before the internet and instantaneous global communications. The only difference is that they will have to do it faster than ever before – and at low cost with high quality – and a number of survival skills are especially important.

Five crucial survival skills

- Traditional law firms must become more capable of facilitating continuous changes, big and small; not just once, but again and again.
- Law firm leaders must be willing to provide direction, business and professional context, feedback and resources to facilitate change, without over-controlling change initiatives and innovative responses.
- In order consistently to deliver high-quality and extraordinary value, law firms will need to align internal capabilities with evolving business realities.
- The more change-ready a law firm and its people become, the faster and better they will be at anticipating and even getting in front of new realities in their client base in a competitive environment.
- Law firms must adopt a longer-term investment mentality for their businesses and their people, rather than a short-term focus on money in the partners' pockets at the end of the year.

In the old days, a goal was a kind of performance straightjacket, used to lock a lawyer into a stated financial commitment to the firm. Now a business plan or a strategic goal does more than offer a financial forecast. It provides the information, documentation, and tools that partners and others in law firms need to respond confidently when they have to move faster, realign resources, shift priorities, and communicate with each other about complex realities. Partners find that the execution of well-thought-out goals, even if delegated to others, is now a dynamic process, not driven by a static performance marker. The process of setting and achieving goals, especially financial ones, will require a never-ending state of intellectual vigilance and collaboration, from more than just an individual partner, for a law firm to stay competitive and profitable.

2.1 Information and knowledge

At every level in a change-ready law firm, members pay attention to the basics. This includes everything from revising strategic priorities, confirming the fundamental purpose of the law firm's services and updating partnership agreements, to listening to their people, developing core business values and skills, writing realistic business plans, analysing and responding to client feedback, clarifying evolving performance expectations and addressing underperformance. The day-to-day discipline of observing the basics provides the stability and flexibility needed to react swiftly to changing expectations and dynamics and to be ready to analyse and use the six classic drivers of law firm profitability in new and insightful ways.

To be change-ready, a law firm also must be aware, externally and internally. This requires closer attention to the economic, political, and social trends that are changing clients' businesses and, in turn, their needs for legal services. All of these forces can have profound consequences for the current profitability of a law firm and whether it can be sustained into the future. Trends involving lawyers' expectations, aspirations and capabilities cannot be ignored, either.

One can always respond better to challenges that are anticipated, or at least foreseen as possibilities, than to surprises. Unfortunately, too many traditional law firms are being surprised by foreseeable changes in the legal services industry and don't react until it is too late.

"One can always respond better to challenges that are anticipated, or at least foreseen as possibilities, than to surprises."

"Ignorance of the changing realities is bad enough. Being aware of them but assuming that they will somehow affect your competitors but will not harm a 'fine old legal institution like ours' is like signing your own death warrant."

Change-ready law firms are never satisfied that they know enough. Although past successes can be instructive in meeting future challenges, these law firms do not overly rely on them as solutions that are still valid. Instead, they constantly seek new information from many sources. This includes:

- listening to and learning from the younger lawyers and staff, as well as people with diverse views, in order to keep everyone engaged;
- generating client feedback and market intelligence; and
- aggressively linking external economic conditions and internal profitability data to business planning.

Change-ready firms constantly test their own assumptions and take nothing for granted. They know that if they rely on a wait-and-see response to an opportunity or a threat, it will be too late to act. Instead, these law firms expect change and anticipate action. A disrupted legal services market does not give second chances.

In many change-challenged law firms, lawyers, staff, and even partners do not know how they can or should contribute to the profitability and financial strength of the firm. In order to contribute to the best of their ability, members of the firm need the resources, tools and skills to keep each other informed, assess risks, identify optional solutions, and measure and evaluate both qualitative and quantitative results. They will benefit from discussing the probabilities of what their jobs or professional responsibilities might look like in the future and even where the firm and its current client base are headed.

Everyone in the firm needs to have an idea of how profits are made and – doubly important – how they can be lost, especially relating to their individual and collective roles and responsibilities. They need to know what questions to ask and answer with regard to their financial planning and contributions. When they are actively involved in setting realistic targets for themselves and their teams, they can play offensively with regard to goal achievement. With relevant information, guidance, and permission to test assumptions – not just once a year in a formal planning or goal-setting process, but continuously – they can take the initiative in stretching and revising financial targets and taking advantage of opportunities.

With adequate, practical information the person or team doing the work can be in the best position, perhaps of anyone in the firm, to assess rapidly and accurately the gaps between financial aspirations and realistic internal capabilities – a key piece of information in a fluid business environment.

Good strategic and business planning methods harness the fundamentals of sustainable profitability and the ambiguities of change in an informed, collaborative environment. When members of the firm – partners, lawyers, managers and staff – are in the financial loop; when they know how to contribute and see a connection between their successful efforts and how they are treated in the firm, financially and otherwise; then they will build and sustain a competitive firm – their firm – together.

2.2 Clear internal communications

Planning and performance take into account the changing realities of the economic environment in which law firms practice. Law firms that continue to follow a do-it-yourself approach, conjuring up strategic plans and performance goals internally, without any relevant external input, become more and more isolated from reality. Imposing unrealistic performance expectations to try to stimulate the productivity of lawyers, sometimes through fear, usually backfires.

Ignorance of the changing realities is bad enough. Being aware of them but assuming that they will somehow affect your competitors but will not harm a "fine old legal institution like ours" is like signing your own death warrant.

Partners often say that the firm's success is a group effort. Yet without a conscious effort to do otherwise, they may approach profitability and other financial aspects of the business in a way that sends a different message entirely. Traditionally, for a variety of reasons, many firms attempted to operate with:

- limited financial transparency;
- irregular or ineffective financial reporting;
- few measurements for partners and lawyers to use as financial markers or targets; and even
- secretive "black box" procedures for remuneration.

One of the results has been that people in the firm, even at the partnership level, end up operating in silos, doing their individual work well enough but with no shared sense of joint contribution or responsibility towards the firm's financial success or even its future.

Change-ready firms are re-examining how they educate others and communicate about their business internally. Passive compliance may sound tempting sometimes; but partners in successful firms already know that it will not stimulate the kind of informed collaboration and commitment they need to compete. A real challenge for partners is to evaluate honestly their current financial practices and culture.

"The fluid, dynamic legal environment of today demands involved and committed people working together, at all levels and across groups in every firm."

Questions for evaluating financial practices and culture
- What is the financial acumen we want our developing lawyers to acquire?
- What financial information would be helpful for them to have, at different stages of their development, and why?
- How can we incentivise a financial mindset in all members of the firm?
- What information do partners need in order to develop well-informed business forecasts and plans?
- What do our partners and firm members need to learn in order to be change-ready?

2.3 A motivating work environment

Beyond knowing *what* to do, people must also feel motivated to contribute. A law firm culture that rewards people for keeping their heads low and their mouths shut will kill what it takes for partners and others to respond confidently in imperfect and often unpredictable conditions. On the other hand, a law firm culture that builds leadership capacity will be change-ready.

People at all levels in the firm need to gain experience, knowledge and skills so they can become adept and confident at spotting problems and opportunities, making decisions and leading change efforts – from big to small. A change-ready law firm does this very specifically by encouraging people to:

- ask and answer informed, thought-provoking questions;
- discuss their differences; and
- solve problems together.

Such a firm makes a point of promoting and rewarding both individual and team performance, because the fluid, dynamic legal environment of today demands involved and committed people working together, at all levels and across groups in every firm.

It becomes obvious that partners cannot expect to initiate, control and manage every response to change that will happen in their firms. Their better role is to provide direction and guidance, to confront problems and take action, not necessarily to solve the problem but to define expectations and preferred outcomes. Partners are in the best position to make sure that they and others have the strategic context, resources, tools and skill development to be change-ready.

With this recognition comes the responsibility to make an investment in the development and preparation of both themselves and their people. For example, lawyers may be working cross-culturally with clients in situations in which a single wrong move or decision could erode trust and adversely affect a client relationship. Lawyers need to be able to come together spontaneously across practice groups to meet client expectations for a seamless response to a complex matter. Politically charged geopolitics may affect the composure and sense of urgency of clients, resulting in negative stress for them and their professional service providers.

Anticipating probabilities is essential practice in a change-ready firm. Partners can draw on the insight, views and experiences of the members of the law firm to find the gaps between their current capabilities (technical, legal and non-technical) and where they need to be, in all probability, to compete successfully, now and into the future.

Without confidence in the judgement and capabilities of the members of their firm, partners end up trying to do it all themselves. By not delegating client relationship management tasks, for example, they perpetuate a downward spiral, in which lawyers do not get the growth opportunities and leadership responsibilities they need to be change-ready; this, in turn, increases frustration for everyone.

Change builds on change. Previous positive experience with implementing change builds confidence, skills and trust. Firm members may still find they get frustrated or even overwhelmed by new expectations, but they rebound more quickly, which increases the odds of successful change in the future. When team members have mastered a new process for sharing client information, for example, they can build on this network of relationships and information for the next change requirement.

Change-ready law firms have also learned that partners reward committed and innovative efforts, even if the net results fall short of the immediate target. They know that attempts at continuous improvement are almost always better than behaviours like finger-pointing, running for cover, or hiding below the radar when things go wrong.

2.4 Raising the bar for leadership

A message especially for law firm partners:
No more shooting the messenger!

Quality practices do not thrive in professional work places that discourage innovation. Nor do they prosper when partners fail to seek out and really listen to diverse viewpoints and new ideas.

It is said that you can't teach an old dog new tricks. Older partners, however, have demonstrated that they can learn new skills of business acumen, emotional intelligence and managing change. At the same time, they do need to heed the admonition in another old adage: "Lead, follow or get out of the way."

Sometimes partners block needed change because of other concerns. They may resist challenging the behaviour of a senior partner for fear of damaging the relationship or showing disrespect. They may carry mental and emotional resentment from unresolved past and current situations into discussions with their partners. The partnership dynamics may be dysfunctional, causing partners to avoid sensitive issues or to resist making decisions until a crisis has arrived. Their demanding schedules may have contributed to developing a bad habit of simply putting out fires, reacting to situations or problems instead of anticipating the need for change and planning it. Whatever the reasons, when partners are not able to lead change in their firms, they risk their own professional futures and those of many others.

Raising the bar for leadership involves consciously documenting, developing and reinforcing the leadership standards, practices, and values that will ensure your firm's future success. Leadership requirements generally are changing rapidly in law firms; nevertheless, they are unique to each firm. Asking for professional, external assistance to redefine and assess leadership skills, issues and situations that pose potential risks to your firm's change readiness represents a strength in the partnership, not a limitation.

Future leaders of the firm, the developing lawyers, take their cues from the top. A lot is at stake. Developing lawyers will pattern themselves after the actions of the partners, for better or worse.

Even when lawyers have good role models, they will need much more to develop into the future leaders of a 21st-century law firm. For example, they need feedback to understand their strengths and limitations in both technical and non-technical areas of their professional life. They need opportunities for increasing levels of leadership responsibility, to gain experience and confidence and to build internal and external networks.

Developing lawyers need attention from partners to build a sense of their professional identity, to negotiate ethical grey areas, to learn how to handle mistakes, and to develop their leadership capabilities. Mentoring, coaching, meaningful interactions with clients, formal and

"Even well-intentioned statements of praise or commendation come across as superficial and are ineffectual if leadership actions are not congruent with verbal messages of praise."

informal feedback, training and professional development – these are the experiences lawyers need now, regularly, to participate successfully in change-challenged law firms and to grow into more formal leadership roles for the future. Each one of these lawyers has a clearly demonstrated effect on the ability of a law firm to build and sustain higher levels of financial performance and profitability, and on the collective culture of the firm.

The need to be change-ready is especially great among younger partners and senior lawyers. In many firms, they will be the ones who will inherit and have to manage the challenges of sustainable profitability. Their ability to act as change leaders will have a direct influence on whether they will succeed or whether, despite their best efforts, their law firms will become extinct.

Change readiness is not just an issue for them, however. Every time a law firm considers whether to admit one of their lawyers to partnership, new questions need to be asked and new criteria weighed, ones that go far beyond the traditional ones about billable hours and the origination of new clients.

Questions to ask when admitting new partners
- How have individuals overcome adversity in their own lives?
- What has been their typical reaction to negative stress or adversity?
- Do they attempt to confront sensitive issues or emotional challenges; or are they more likely to respond passively to problem situations and the need for change?
- What is their approach to getting things done and solving problems; and what skills do they demonstrate in doing so?
- To what extent do they anticipate obstacles or roadblocks, and help others to do so?
- How sound is their judgement in evaluating and responding to professional and client service risks?
- To what extent have they learned from their mistakes?
- How well can they assess their own strengths and limitations? Are they able to see themselves as others see them?

These are all indicators about whether lawyers have the leadership competencies to manage their own performance and work together with others in a dynamic environment to make changes successful – not just once, but time and time again. Self-awareness, self-confidence, empathy, conflict management, optimism, and other non-technical skills represent the emotional intelligence capital of the firm. They are all skills that can, and should be, reinforced in the firm through modelling, development, feedback and practical experience, well before a lawyer is considered for promotion to partner.

"Showing a willingness to learn and the courage to ask for and use constructive feedback are two of the most powerful things partners can do to build a better firm and to send a message to the people in their firm that they care – about each of them, the business, and the clients."

2.5 Becoming the change you want to see

Partners set a visible example that others will emulate. In a very real sense, they must be the change that they want to see in their firm and in their peers, lawyers and staff. Showing a willingness to learn and the courage to ask for and use constructive feedback are two of the most powerful things partners can do to build a better firm and to send a message to the people in their firm that they care – about each of them, the business, and the clients.

Confronting problems and taking actions to improve or reset the *status quo*, even if these actions are executed step-by-step over a period of time, says, "We care about our shared future together." The opposite is true when partners – consciously or unconsciously – avoid resolving ongoing problems, scapegoat others in the firm for those problems, and show a reluctance to use feedback to better understand their own strengths and limitations as change leaders. Even well-intended statements of praise or commendation come across as superficial and are ineffectual if leadership actions are not congruent with verbal messages of praise.

Responding to the need for continuous change – and learning how to facilitate the process of change in law firms – requires that everyone in the firm engage in the business, a domain traditionally controlled by the partners and senior management of the firm. Partners' comfort zones, their leadership skills, and their traditional investment mentality about developing people in the firm will likely be challenged. Yet, without their leadership, critical thinking and analysis, and ongoing involvement, any meaningful response to the need for change is doomed. As in any other business or profession, when the market is disrupted, a firm that is not genuinely change-ready – from the senior partners to the most junior staff – will be swept away.

3. Paradigm shifts in the legal services industry

How can a traditional profession, which has relied largely on 200-year-old assumptions about how legal services should be delivered to clients, respond to the changes that are disrupting legal markets worldwide? The first step is to understand the concept of paradigms and to be alert to paradigm shifts when they happen.

3.1 The future is here, but many of us don't know it

Technology has been a fundamental component of the practice of law for a quarter-century; but most law firms have failed to understand how it is fundamentally changing – indeed, already has fundamentally changed – the practice of law.

No one can deny that the business of practising law will probably be much more challenging 10 years from now than it is even today; and that the seismic changes that technology has introduced into the business world will contribute to that challenge – operationally, ethically, financially and strategically. Law firms will have to continue to evolve. Not all will be able to do so.

The ever-faster pace of change has blurred the perceptions of law firm owners, leaders, and managers. It is like trying to study a high-speed train passing close by at 300 kph.

> **The law firm of the future: key points**
> - **The future is already here.** The forces that will shape your professional future are already present in today's legal markets. The problem is that many law firms can't see them.
> - **The legal profession is being subjected to multiple paradigm shifts.** Even the most successful law firms often can't see these forces because they do not understand the force and effect of paradigms in the practice of law. The profession is in fact a forest of paradigms, and many lawyers can spend a whole career in the practice of law without ever noticing them until they feel the tremors of declining financial performance, and sometimes even not then.
> - **Just thinking about the future is not enough.** Law firms must start moving now towards the future that they want. "Wait and see" might seem prudent in the face of bewildering change. Maybe it is better, one wants to think, to wait until everything gets sorted out, until some of the dust settles. That might appeal to the risk-averse orientation that most lawyers assume when advising their clients; but it inevitably leaves a law firm with fewer options and a higher risk of bad decisions and ineffective responses.
> - **You can and should build your own future.** In addition to investing time and intellectual energy in trying to anticipate and understand the future, there is an equally important need for law firm leaders and planners to understand what they need to do to become the law firm of the future they aspire to be.

3.2 Understanding paradigms

Why is it that lawyers and law firms are so often surprised? Why do so many law firms always seem to be playing catch-up with their clients and the business world in general?

Undoubtedly one of the biggest obstacles to law firms' ability to respond to change is the effect of the paradigms that have governed the way that they conceptualise and understand the practice of law. The word paradigm comes from the Greek παράδειγμα, which means an example, model or pattern. Paradigms are mental assumptions that we make, based on our experiences in the world, which not only govern our actions in certain situations, but can also shape the way that we perceive them. A paradigm can even cause us to fail to perceive things that we otherwise see clearly.

Some of the traditional paradigms of the profession seem almost laughable today, but they were articles of faith for most law firms only 20 years ago.

Past paradigms of the legal profession
- We will never get lawyers to use computers.
- Law firm websites are just another form of advertising.
- The hourly rate is the most profitable fee structure for law firms.
- Word processing and document assembly will kill creativity in the practice of law and hurt professional quality.
- Most clients expect face-to-face contact.
- The traditional law firm is the best structure for delivering quality legal services.
- Lawyers and accountants can never be partners in a professional services firm.
- Social media is a waste of time for law firms.

"These intellectual frameworks can sometimes lead to important insights, but the most effective responses to the challenges of the future are usually the ones that honestly and squarely address the economics, professional culture and competitive context of individual law firms."

Three principles of paradigms have been particularly troublesome for law firms, as well as other industries and professions:

- **Paradigm shifts usually begin outside one's profession, not within it.** Sometimes the best ideas come from what might appear to be the most unlikely sources. This is why most proponents of a new paradigm are initially viewed as disloyal, or worse, within their own organisations.
- **Paradigm shifts begin before they are noticed or needed.** Firms that notice and respond to paradigm shifts first can achieve substantial competitive advantage.
- **When a paradigm shifts, everything resets to zero.** Past success does not ensure future survival. Some of the most impressive exhibits in a museum of failed businesses would be those that failed to see a paradigm shift in their industry or, even worse, saw it and tried to ignore it.

Even to perceive the future of the legal profession, much less actually to understand it, we must be willing to escape many of the paradigms that have shaped the practice of law for centuries, and which can prevent us from seeing new realities. As futurist Joel Barker has said, "The role of leadership is to find, recognize, and secure the future."[21]

"Many traditional law firms hold onto delusional notions that clients will simply keep coming to them for their needs because of their name and past glories."

Most of what passes for innovation in the legal profession is little more than adjustments to the *status quo*. These quick fixes might work well for a while, but they usually do not respond to basic changes in client expectations and the nature of the competition, which are shaping the future.

In an era of shifting paradigms and growing intolerance by clients of fake innovation in law firms, it is natural to look for and cling to so-called "best practice", or academic models for strategic planning. Although there is much to be learned from the business world beyond the legal profession, as well as from academic perspectives, each law firm is a unique system. These intellectual frameworks can sometimes lead to important insights, but the most effective responses to the challenges of the future are usually the ones that honestly and squarely address the economics, professional culture and competitive context of individual law firms – not only as they are now but as they will evolve, in all probability, into the future.

4. Is your law firm trudging silently towards oblivion?

Do the cultures of traditional law firms make them incapable of change, as many observers suggest? What are the qualities and characteristics we can observe in those law firms that are trudging silently into oblivion, compared to those who are turning their lives around?

Just as banks did prior to the 1980s, many traditional law firms hold onto delusional notions that clients will simply keep coming to them for their needs because of their name and past glories. Their leaders are committed to maintaining the *status quo* and waiting for a return to the good old days when they took growth and revenue for granted. Some want to tweak the edges for appearances' sake, trying to look and act differently. Yet silently they want to keep the same old culture and way of doing things. Others pine for the days when a strong managing partner took care of everything so that the other lawyers could get on with practising law. Still others truly want to achieve different results, but by telling others to behave differently while they remain the same. However, when a paradigm shifts and disrupts an industry, everything resets to zero.

Change-ready law firms demonstrate their capabilities every day. They figure out how to anticipate the changes that need to be made and make the necessary decisions. They grasp the complex conditions around them, both internally and externally. They develop clear priorities and plan their actions according to their best in-the-moment knowledge and informed perceptions of their clients, their competition and the economic realities of their practices, as well as a sound grasp of their internal culture, its assets and capabilities; and they backfill that information constantly. Finally, they execute with both the intellectual discipline and flexibility required to make adjustments pay.[22]

Being change-ready sounds relatively straightforward. But too many law firms continue to fall down on implementation of these commonsense practices, and for those firms the future is bleak.

5. Playing a poor hand well

Robert Louis Stevenson wrote: "Life is not so much a matter of holding good cards, but sometimes of playing a poor hand well."

The firms that will thrive in the 21st century are not necessarily those that have held good cards in the past. Success will come to the firms that know how to reframe the risks and adversities of today in new ways, so they can play their hands well. The choices are theirs to make.

Law firms have the capability to continue to evolve in response to changing environments. The question for their lawyers is whether they will look at the comet blazing across the twilight skies as a call to change or, like the dinosaurs, continue trudging on, telling themselves that none of it will affect them.

Notes

1 Sarah Kessler, "One. That's how many careers automation has eliminated in the last 60 years", World Economic Forum, 27 March 2017, available at:
www.weforum.org/agenda/2017/03/automation-has-totally-eliminated-just-one-career-in-the-last-60-years. But see Ernesto Londoño, "Rio de Janeiro Elevator Attendants 'Adore' Their Dying, Chatty Trade", *New York Times*, 25 November 2018, available at:
www.nytimes.com/2018/11/25/world/americas/brazil-rio-de-janeiro-elevator-attendants.html.
2 James Manyika *et al*, "Harnessing automation for a future that works", McKinsey Global Institute, January 2017, available at: www.mckinsey.com/global-themes/digital-disruption/harnessing-automation-for-a-future-that-works.
3 Brian Sheppard, "Incomplete Innovation and the Premature Disruption of Legal Services", *Mich St L Rev* 1797, 1806 (2015). See also Farhad Manjoo, "Will Robots Steal Your Job? Software Could Kill Lawyers. Why That's Good for Everyone Else", SLATE, 29 September 2011, available at:
www.slate.com/articles/technology/robot_invasion/2011/09/will_robots_steal_your_job_5.html.
4 Thomas S Clay and Eric A Seeger, *Law Firms In Transition* 2018, Altman Weil Inc, 2018, pp ii–iii.
5 The legal services industry can be divided, for purposes of this discussion, into two general sectors: commercial and retail. The retail sector delivers legal services, usually at low cost or on a contingency-fee basis to individual clients and small businesses, in areas such as family law, criminal law, conveyancing, small estates and trusts, and business law issues for small enterprises. This sector has remained relatively price insensitive due to several factors, including the relative inexperience and lack of sophistication of the clients as purchasers of legal services and the high-volume, somewhat standardised nature of the services and products. The commercial legal services sector serves larger corporate and institutional clients and high net-worth private clients in high-value or complex matters.
Many law firms, especially small and midsize firms, have a mixture of retail and commercial clients, but most firms are oriented primarily to one sector or the other. Whether a law firm has predominantly a retail or a commercial practice can affect how the firm is structured and operates and, as a result, can influence the factors that are most influential in the firm's profitability.
6 Predatory pricing is the practice of offering relatively sophisticated legal work, such as in mergers and acquisitions or anti-trust matters, at prices that are far below the prevailing range of fee quotations in the market, in the hope of winning market share from better-known, established competitors.
7 A 90% recording realisation means that only 90% of the billable work that is performed is recorded. If only 90% of the recorded work is billed to the client, this reduces the overall realisation to 81% of the work performed (90% × 90% = 81%). If only 90% of the billed fees are collected, this reduces overall realisation to 72.9% (81% × 90% = 72.9%).
8 In fact, in most firms, staffing leverage ratios never really did reflect the actual workings of a firm or practice group. Even today, in many firms that appear to have a "healthy" staffing ratio of one partner to four or five associates, partners nonetheless fail to delegate as much work to associates as they should; and when they do delegate, they may be so unskilled in managing the delegated work that unclear instructions, and the need for back-and-forth rework, make the delegation less profitable than had the partner simply done the work him- or herself (an option which is already unprofitable in most instances).
9 As of 1 December 2018, the database for the Walker Clark Strategic Business Development Survey included 6,623 respondents.
10 In fact, this factor scored so far above the other 20 indicators that after six years of including it as a quality indicator in their research, the authors stopped asking about it.
11 The other 15 quality indicators, in order of priority according to respondents, are:
• Important:
  ◦ Reputations of individual lawyers
  ◦ Respect for budget
  ◦ Reputation of the law firm
  ◦ Partner supervision
  ◦ Resolution of disputes with clients
  ◦ Delegation of legal work
  ◦ Progress reports
  ◦ Innovation in cost control
  ◦ Accurate and complete invoices
• Secondary:
  ◦ Government relations
  ◦ Low price
  ◦ Relationships with other firms
  ◦ Introduction of new business relationships
  ◦ Diversity
• Unimportant:
  ◦ Convenient office location
12 Modelled profitability estimates the profits produced by each partner or a partner's book of business, based on factors such as fee collections and fully loaded operating cost.

13 This comment is limited to the present example only. It is not intended, and should not be inferred, to be a recommendation by the authors or a suggestion of a benchmark or best practice for law firms.

14 The authors suggest these limits, based on their observations and experience, as general guidelines to detect variation beyond the limits of normal variation in a work process. Any measurements above or below these suggested limits are usually, but certainly not always, indicators of a potential issue in the way that a law firm prepares, produces, and delivers legal services and products. The better method, of course, is to identify values that are outside the normal limits of variation based on actual performance data from a particular law firm or a practice group within a law firm.

15 This is a conservative estimate for most partners in both commercial and retail law firms. In some practice areas, such as litigation, the opportunity might be greater.

16 Some law firms might reduce this value to reflect overhead per partner hour; but the authors do not recommend this adjustment because it dilutes the productivity aspect of this planning method by introducing the concept of profitability per hour. The intellectually clearer way to plan and manage individual productivity is to focus on time spent and revenue produced.

17 This is a conservative value, used only for purposes of this example. In the absence of actual data of the revenue return on the investment of time in business development, which few firms have traditionally compiled, it is better to apply a conservative factor and adjust it as actual data is developed. In the authors' experience, the measured return on investment in developing new business from current or recent clients has ranged from 8-to-1 to 16-to-1, but the specific characteristics of the practice groups and the services they delivered, combined with the small number of cases observed, make it impossible to establish a general credible benchmark for all firms and practice groups.

18 These allocated operating costs would probably be significantly higher in order to pay for the advanced systems used in firm B, but the difference allocated on a per-associate basis probably would not significantly affect the total allocated operating costs per associate, except in small law firms. The difference in profitability as between the two firms would still be dramatic.

19 It does not matter, for purposes of this example, whether the firm bills the associate's time on an hourly rate or uses this value per hour as the basis for calculating a fixed fee in a matter that includes the associate's participation.

20 See W Edwards Deming, *Out of the Crisis*, MIT–CAES, 1986 and *The New Economics*, MIT–CAES, 1994. In *Out of the Crisis*, Deming advocated 14 points for improved management and financial performance. Four points are especially relevant to the ability of a traditional law firm to sustain its profitability in a disrupted legal services industry:

• Create constancy of purpose for improvement of products and services.
• Improve constantly and forever every process for planning, production, and service. Improve quality and productivity, and thus constantly decrease costs.
• Adopt and institute leadership. The aim of supervision should be to help people and machines and gadgets to do a better job.
• Drive out fear so that everyone may work effectively for the company because they want it to succeed.

21 See Joel Arthur Barker, *Five Regions of the Future: Preparing Your Business for Tomorrow's Technology Revolution*, Penguin, 2005. See also www.joelbarker.com.

22 See Lisa M Walker Johnson, "From Strategic Planning to Strategic Success: the '3x3' Model", the Walker Clark World View blog, 8 April 2017, available at: www.walkerclark.com/worldview-blog/previous-worldview-posts/269-from-strategic-planning-to-strategic-success.html; and *Implementing Strategic Priorities in the Legal Profession*, Walker Clark LLC, 2017, available at: www.walkerclark.com/images/documents/publications/Walker_Johnson_Strategic_Implementation _in_the_Legal_Profession_04-17.pdf.

About the authors

Norman K Clark
Founding principal, Walker Clark LLC
norman.clark@walkerclark.com

Norman K Clark is the managing principal of the international legal management consultancy Walker Clark LLC, which he helped to found in 2002. His consulting practice specialises in issues of strategic planning and implementation, law firm profitability, governance and quality assurance.

His 45-year career as a lawyer includes experience as a trial lawyer, trial judge, law professor and senior manager of the delivery of legal services on a global scale. He has been a full-time business adviser to the legal profession for the past 23 years, having advised clients in law firms and corporate and government law departments in more than 60 countries on five continents.

Norman holds a BSc, a JD and an LLM. He is a retired member of the Pennsylvania Bar, a past chair of the International Bar Association Law Firm Management Committee, and a co-chair of the American Bar Association Cross-Border Practice Management Committee.

Lisa M Walker Johnson
Founding principal, Walker Clark LLC
lisa.walkerjohnson@walkerclark.com

Lisa Walker Johnson's professional background is as a counselling psychologist, with more than 30 years' experience in senior levels of business management and consulting to corporations and law firms worldwide.

As a psychologist with deep experience in law firm management issues, Lisa helps law firms to manage sensitive and frequently difficult change management issues, such as the integration and retention of lateral partners, leadership transitions between generations of partners, cultural due diligence during mergers, and the implementation of strategic change in the disruptive business environments confronting the legal services industry.

Lisa has published extensively in these areas and frequently speaks about them at major international conferences for legal professionals.